Recent Alumni and Higher Education

Recent Alumni and Higher Education

A SURVEY OF COLLEGE GRADUATES

by *Joe L. Spaeth*

*Associate Program Director, National Opinion
Research Center, University of Chicago*

and *Andrew M. Greeley*

Program Director, NORC

with a commentary by *Theodore M. Hesburgh*, CSC

A General Report Prepared for
The Carnegie Commission on Higher Education

MCGRAW-HILL BOOK COMPANY
*New York   St. Louis   San Francisco   Düsseldorf
London   Sydney   Toronto   Mexico   Panama*

The Carnegie Commission on Higher Education,
1947 Center Street, Berkeley, California 94704,
has sponsored preparation of this report as a
part of a continuing effort to obtain and present
significant information for public discussion.
The views expressed are those of the authors.

RECENT ALUMNI AND HIGHER EDUCATION
A Survey of College Graduates

Library of Congress catalog card number 70-119830
123456789 MAMM 79876543210
10012

Foreword

Efforts to solve or circumvent the campus crisis of the moment often claim so much of the college educator's attention that a longer view is neglected. Often neglected, too—at least until the next fund drive—is news of the whereabouts and progress of recent alumni. This is unfortunate since they, of all persons, are especially qualified by experience to contribute insight into the ways in which college failed or served them and perhaps how it may best serve the future.

For nearly a decade, sociologists Joe L. Spaeth and Andrew M. Greeley, with colleagues at the National Opinion Research Center (NORC) in Chicago, have conducted surveys of the alumni who were members of the class of 1961. Naturally, we turned to them to obtain alumni perspectives on matters relevant to concerns of the Carnegie Commission on Higher Education. Another study then was initiated by NORC, partly to discover answers to questions that seemed to us significant.

The authors and the Commission wanted to know how members of the class of 1961, now well settled in their careers and many with children for whose higher education they had begun to plan, assessed the performance of their alma mater. How closely, for example, had alumni lives and careers matched their early aspirations? Looking back across seven years, would they have preferred a different kind of college program? What courses would they now want to take? What were their ideas on curriculum reform? How loyal were they to their alma mater? Did they contribute to fund drives? For what reasons? How did they feel toward today's campus activists? Had their political affiliations changed much? If so, how? The findings are the subject of this report.

As the authors point out, the normal procedure for survey researchers, after presenting their data, is "to fold their tables

v

and quietly steal away." Breaking with this tradition, Dr. Spaeth and Dr. Greeley tell us what they see as the significance of their findings. There are surprises. Administrators of some institutions may be disturbed by the views of these recent graduates, while others will find in them reassurances that their college has been on the right track. Whatever the response, it is our hope that this study will provide a better understanding of the contributions the colleges can make to their students.

Clark Kerr
Chairman
The Carnegie Commission
on Higher Education

February, 1970

Preface

This report is the outgrowth of the fortunate conjunction of the National Opinion Research Center's longitudinal study of 1961 college graduates with the Carnegie Commission on Higher Education. Dr. Clark Kerr, chairman of the Commission, was interested in the views of recent alumni on several important issues related to higher education—loyalty to one's college, reactions to one's college education, and attitudes toward financing higher education. NORC wanted to carry out another wave, the fifth, of a study that had started in 1961 and had been continued through 1964.[1] We also thought that the issues raised by the Commission were interesting and important. (This is not always the reaction of survey researchers to the concerns of a potential client.)

There is no doubt that our hopes were fulfilled. The data produced by this wave have greatly enriched the entire study. We hope that the Carnegie Commission has benefited equally.

It is conventional for coauthors to assert that theirs was a true collaboration to which each contributed equally. In our instance, the conventional utterance happens to be true. This report would have been a poorer one if it had not been for our mutual discussion, criticism, and education. Nonetheless, there was a division of labor. Spaeth was responsible for drafting Chapters 1 and 7 to 9; Greeley was responsible for Chapters 2 to 6. Chapter 10 was our joint responsibility and reflects the views of both of us. Spaeth is the senior author because he was also responsible for administering the study.

[1] Data collection and preparation for the first four waves were supported through the Cooperative Research Program of the Office of Education, U.S. Department of Health, Education and Welfare, under contract SAE-9102, and by the National Institute of Mental Health under grants M5615, M5615-02, M5615-03, M5615-04, and M5615-05.

Only the names of the authors of a report appear on the title page. At NORC, many other people contribute to the successful realization of a project. Bette Hayes Passin supervised the locating of respondents (we had lost track of them for four years), the mailing of questionnaires to them, and the following up on those who did not respond promptly. The success of her endeavors is signalized by the response rate of over 80 percent. Nancy Morrison and Edward I. Weston performed the necessary data-processing operations that provided us with data to analyze. Nancy McCready searched the questionnaires to find the quotations that are used in Chapters 4 and 5, and Ellen Fried checked all the tables. Nella V. Siefert did her usual fine job in typing the first draft, and Nancy Nagel produced an impeccable final manuscript. Mary A. Spaeth gave her usual efficient performance as NORC's editor. Norman M. Bradburn provided sage advice throughout, and Larry H. Litten made several sets of cogent criticisms of the various drafts.

We should also mention the peculiar NORC institution known as a "Group Mind," in which a group of one's colleagues takes a questionnaire draft and cuts it to ribbons. After the researchers' egos have been put back together and the questionnaire has been rewritten, the questionnaire is much improved.

Last, but really first, we must thank the alumni who responded to our questionnaire. This is the fifth such document that they have filled out for us. Such devotion is light-years above and beyond the call of duty.

Joe L. Spaeth
Andrew M. Greeley

Contents

List of Figures

List of Tables

Recent Alumni and Higher Education

1. The Class of 1961

A 1961 college graduate remembers his college as quite a different place from the one he sees on television. In 1961, politically motivated student disruption was virtually unheard of. Admitted during the years of Eisenhower apathy, the member of the class of 1961 was about to graduate by the time the Kennedy civil rights movement was taking shape. Since then, the movement has waxed and waned and has been replaced by Black Power and Black Separatism. Vietnam has raised an entirely new set of issues. And both racism and the actions of the military-industrial complex have moved, as sources of concern, from somewhere "out there" to become foci of direct relevance to a college or university.

Today, radical students castigate the urban university for its behavior as a landlord and for its failure, its reluctance, or its slowness to provide special programs for blacks and members of other minorities. They rebel against it for training officers for the military, for aiding recruitment to various branches of the military-industrial complex, and for carrying out research for the Defense Department. Today's students have brought the major social problems onto the campus and then added a few of their own. In the span of two college generations, the tenor of campus life has undergone a complete transformation.

Reactions of recent alumni to these developments is one of the concerns of this book. The politization of American campuses is the most dramatic development that has taken place in higher education since the class of '61 graduated. In fact, it is possible that higher education may become a wedge that splits the American polity.

A recent Gallup poll (1969) has shown that the political and social views of today's college students are as vehemently rejected by the general public as are traditional views by the students.

Considerable evidence has accumulated which indicates that the public is increasingly likely to sanction repressive measures against colleges, faculties, and students. From this situation it is easy to conclude that the current financial crisis in higher education will only be heightened in the future. Militant and other programs of change may be driving American higher education down the road to the poorhouse, where the public and its representatives stand ready to open the doors.

Nonetheless, some segments of the general public are less hostile than others to student concerns. In particular, persons who themselves have gone to college are closer to the views of students than are those with less education. Among alumni, the younger ones are even more likely to be in sympathy with the protests (Spaeth, 1969).

Young but not new alumni are therefore an important part of higher education's constituency. It is possible that they might serve as a bridge across the generation gap. In addition, they will be called on by their colleges for financial and other forms of support. They will be sending children of their own to college. And taxes applicable to higher education may represent a significant portion of their rather sizable tax bills.

To what extent have student protests caused a decline in alumni support? How *do* relatively recent alumni feel about these student protests? Do such feelings affect views on other aspects of higher education or feelings of loyalty to one's alma mater? Does the occurrence of a protest on one's old campus change one's feelings toward the place? There is already evidence that donations from big givers have declined as a result of demonstrations. What about the *young* rank and file?

Of course, reactions to student demonstrations are just a single facet of one's orientation to his college. Regardless of his views on student politics, a person's own experiences during college will affect his loyalty to his alma mater. His evaluation of these experiences will depend on how well college met his needs. In other words, people come to college with certain goals in mind, however vague these may be, and the extent to which these goals are met should have considerable bearing on one's willingness to support his college.

Thus, any attempt to assess the relevance of student upheavals requires a broader context. One aspect of this context is alumni perceptions of their own desires and goals and of how well their

college met them. Another is their general perceptions of alma
mater. How good was it? What were *its* goals, and how did they
mesh with those of the student? Such considerations provide a
framework within which to look at alumni reactions to student
militancy and to proposals for general changes in higher education,
and at the level of financial contributions to one's college.

Many of these matters concern the functioning of higher education as a social system. A few of these functions will be discussed
directly. Thus, for example, it is widely held that a college education should produce a person who is interested in and informed
about literature and the arts. One would expect the better colleges
to do a better job of this than the poorer ones. Do they? How interested are college graduates in the humanities? How avidly do they
engage in cultural pursuits?

Another function of higher education is career training. Though
a college education cannot take the place of on-the-job training,
nor should this be expected, many people believe that it prepares
one for elite positions in the labor market. How important a function of college do alumni think career training should be? How
does this preparation actually take place? To what extent do a
person's experiences in college or graduate school change his career
plans?

We shall attempt to answer questions like these with data collected from persons who graduated from college in June, 1961.
These people left when campus politics had more bearing on student government than on the military-industrial complex, and
they entered in the quiet Eisenhower years. Their college experiences are therefore a relatively unlikely source of sympathy for
student militancy, though the relative youth of this group may
leave them open to concern with some of the problems that trouble
the militants.

The study is based on a sample of 40,000 graduates of 135
accredited or large colleges and universities.[1] Data were collected
in 1961, 1962, 1963, 1964, and 1968. The 1968 wave, commissioned by the Carnegie Commission, was devoted to ascertain-
ing the views of alumni on their colleges and higher education
in general. Some of the issues covered have been mentioned above.
This last wave of the study is based on a 30 percent subsample of
respondents who had returned all four previous questionnaires.

---

[1] For details on sample, see Davis (1964).

Of the 6,005 persons drawn, 4,868 returned completed questionnaires; this is a response rate of 81 percent.[2] Of the respondents, 58 percent were male and 42 percent were female.

The class of '61 is approaching the midpoint between two rather significant events—the day they graduated from college and the day their children matriculate. Though they have little doubt that their children will go to college, they are not sure which school, or even what kind of school, their children will attend. The attractions of alma mater are by no means overwhelming.

Seven years after graduation still represents a rather transitional state in the lives of college graduates. Many of the men are only beginning to take up the careers for which they have been preparing, while others went to work right after college and have continued in the labor force ever since.

A college graduating class is a rather diverse group of people. They come from varying backgrounds, graduate from widely different kinds of colleges, and hold a great diversity of values and orientations toward their colleges.

This diversity even extends to such a matter as age. When they graduated, 30 percent were 23 or older; 6 percent were 30 or older. Clearly, a substantial number did not go to and through college on the usual schedule. In fact, 13 percent did not go straight from high school to college, and among those who did not matriculate right after high school, the median delay was about three years. Eighteen percent of this class dropped out and came back; at least they reported leaving college for a term or more.

It is no wonder, then, that a quarter of all graduates were married as seniors and that two-thirds of the married had children. Three years later, in 1964, two-thirds were married, and two-thirds of the married had children. In 1968, over eight in ten were married, and this same proportion of the married had children. The average number of children in an alumnus's family in 1968 was two, with the oldest child averaging between three and four years of age.

Nearly a quarter had met their spouses at their own college, and over a fifth were married to people who had not attended college at all.

---

[2] Data not reported here indicate that the decision to include only respondents returning all questionnaires created minimal nonresponse bias. See Spaeth (forthcoming, Appendix 1). The original sampling design underrepresented graduates of small colleges. Responses reported here have been weighted to take this fact into account.

The educational attainment of this class obviously outstripped that of their parents; only a third of their mothers had even gone to college, as had the fathers of four in ten. About half of the fathers were either professionals, proprietors, managers, or officials. Among the class of '61, 71 percent of those working were in professional positions, and an additional 19 percent were proprietors, managers, or officials, for a total of 90 percent. Ultimately, 73 percent expect to be professionals and 22 percent managers.

A third of these alumni came from families with incomes of at least $10,000 a year (in pre-1960 dollars); even at this early career stage, three-quarters of these alumni were doing as well as their parents had done. But the older generation still surpasses the younger in the proportion with more substantial incomes; 11 percent of the former and 9 percent of the latter were making at least $20,000 annually.

Thirty-five percent had enrolled in graduate school during the year after college, a figure that remained essentially the same during the next two years. By 1968, it had dropped to 17 percent. Three respondents in five had attended graduate school for some period, nearly half for a year or more, and a fifth for at least three years. A third held some kind of higher degree. Twenty-one percent had earned a master's, 10 percent a professional, and only 4 percent a doctoral degree. In contrast, one-sixth said that they planned to earn the doctorate, and over two-thirds reported the intention of earning some kind of advanced degree. Even at this seemingly late date, recent alumni plan to be consumers of higher education.

Recent alumni certainly expect to be consumers of higher education as far as their children are concerned. Ninety-three percent expect all their boys to attend college, and 86 percent expect all their girls to attend. Nearly all expect at least some of their children to attend college. Sixty percent have taken some concrete financial step—such as savings accounts, insurance, investments, or trust funds—to prepare for this eventuality. Ninety-nine percent say that they will make at least some contribution to the financing of their children's education, with nearly half reporting that they will contribute at least three-quarters of a child's expenses. This intention is not formulated in the naïve hope that college costs will decrease. The median parent thinks that the cost of keeping a child in school for a year will be about $3,000.

As a group, parents are far more concerned with the quality of the education their children will get than with how much it may cost. Eighty-two percent said that very high academic standing was of great importance in choosing a college for their children, contrasted with only 12 percent who said the same of low costs. Nearly everyone (98 percent) wanted a college to provide a good general education, 87 percent wanted career training, and 84 percent thought that personality development would be desirable. Only 19 percent thought that it would be desirable that their child go to their own alma mater; most (72 percent) were indifferent on this matter.

When asked in 1968 about their emotional feeling about their college, 27 percent claimed a strong attachment and 85 percent (including the 27 percent already mentioned) said that they liked it. When the same question had been asked at graduation, 32 percent had claimed a strong attachment and 75 percent had said they liked their college. Apparently the years have eroded both strong positive and negative feelings.

Whatever their attachment, 37 percent made a financial contribution to their college in 1967–68. As one might expect of recent alumni, their gifts were rather small. Even among the donors, the median gift was about $10, and only 13 percent had given as much as $50. This is only about 5 percent of all alumni. These data may be extended to the entire class of '61 by multiplying the mean gift by the number of college graduates in that year. In 1967–68, higher education received about $3.5 million from its 1961 college graduates. If they contributed as they expected to do, they gave over $4 million in 1968–69. While those are not inconsiderable sums, they are puny by comparison with what is needed.

Of course alumni, like other taxpayers, will make other contributions. How do they view the financing of higher education in their role as taxpayers? Nearly three in five agree that state taxes should be raised to provide more money for higher education. Forty-five percent agree that *all* colleges should receive federal aid to help cover operating expenses; 61 percent would favor federal aid to institutions with no religious affiliation; only 17 percent favor no federal aid at all. Opinions on state aid are very similar. Forty-one percent favor state aid to all colleges; 61 percent would extend such aid to public and nondenominational institutions.

Alumni tend to feel that financial aid to students should be allocated according to criteria of need and ability. On the average, they think that about 40 percent of all high school graduates are intelligent enough to receive aid. Of course, one should remember that only about half of a high school class goes on to college. While 75 percent would limit aid to needy students, only 17 percent would subsidize all bright ones.

In short, recent alumni seem aware of the problems of financing higher education, concerned that they be solved, willing to undergo at least a mild sacrifice to contribute to their solution, and receptive to government subsidies for schools and students. They intend to pay for much of their own children's college education and are rather realistic about what it will cost. They have already begun to prepare for paying the bills. They would also like to be able to deduct their children's college expenses from their income tax—over 90 percent say they would agree to such a proposal.

When compared with their own parents, the alumni are a liberal group politically. Just over half of the alumni classified themselves as political liberals, while two in five reported that their parents were liberals. At the same time, only 1 percent identified themselves as part of the New Left. Only 5 percent had participated in an antiwar protest and 9 percent in a civil rights protest. But 15 percent would approve if their children protested against the war and 30 percent would approve if their children took part in a civil rights protest. About half thought, in spring, 1968, that "the protests of college students are a healthy sign for America."

Here we have a moderate group tied into the traditional political system but relatively sympathetic to the concerns of their recent successors on campus. How do their views on these matters and their experiences with their own colleges influence their views on higher education?

This report will be in three parts. The first will try to give a detailed answer to the question just asked. The second will discuss some of the ways in which passage through colleges and universities affects the career development of male alumni. The third will attempt to link the first two parts through considerations on the present state of higher education in America.

In the first part, we shall discuss alumni views on the goals of their own colleges, the extent to which college graduates are interested in literature and the arts, evaluations of one's own college, reactions to proposals for the reform of higher education, political and social attitudes, and financial contributions to one's alma mater.

In the second part, we shall investigate the determinants of college entrance, the role of college attendance in career planning, and the role of higher education in changing career plans and affecting actual occupational attainment.

Part One
Alumni Reactions to Their College

2. The Goals of Higher Education

The June, 1961 graduates were given two opportunities to elaborate their feelings about the goals of higher education. They were asked to choose from a list of services what they thought their college should have provided for them, and they were asked to check a list of aims of higher education that they thought were important. In Table 1 we observe that graduates have "liberal" (as opposed to "vocational") expectations of what higher education should do for its students. The goal least frequently mentioned—preparation for marriage and family—found favor with two-fifths of the respondents. The items in Table 1 can be grouped into three categories: the first five—ability to think for oneself, broad knowledge of arts and sciences, tolerance for people and ideas, ability to make one's own decisions, and the formulation of values and goals in life—are endorsed by four-fifths or more of the respondents. The second set of goals—getting ahead in the world, learning to get along with others, and training for present job—are approved by approximately two-thirds of the respondents. The third set of goals—service to others, friendships, and preparation for marriage and family—are approved by three-fifths of the respondents or less. The first category clearly falls within the broad liberal and intellectual tradition of the goals of higher education, while the second and third would be more likely to be part of the tradition that views higher educational goals as practical, either for career advancement or for personality development. There is not much doubt that the liberal goals are more popular with the 1961 graduates, although the vocational goals are not rejected, by any means. Like most other Americans, then, the alumni seem to want the higher educational institution to assume a broad range of responsibilities.

Table 2, which reports alumni evaluation of what "should have

TABLE 1 *Percent responding to the question: "Which of the following do you think your college should have given you?"*

I think my college should have	Percent "yes"
Developed my abilities to think and express myself	98
Given me a broad knowledge of the arts and sciences	90
Expanded my tolerance for people and ideas	90
Helped me to learn how to make my own decisions	81
Helped me to formulate the values and goals of my life	80
Prepared me to get ahead in the world	70
Helped me to learn how to get along with others	67
Trained me for my present job	65
Helped me to learn ways of helping people	60
Helped me to form valuable and lasting friendships	54
Helped prepare me for marriage and family	39

been the aims, intentions, or goals" of their alma mater, merely confirms from a different perspective the findings in Table 1: the liberal or intellectual goals are the most popular. The alumni think that their colleges should have produced a well-rounded student with a cultivated and objective intellect who understands the methods of scholarship and scientific research, whose inner character has been developed, who understands his citizenship responsibilities, and who has been prepared for a useful career. A substantial minority are willing to concede at least "great" importance to training of the good consumer (31 percent).

When the alumni were forced to choose between a general education and a career-oriented education, they overwhelmingly endorsed the idea of a general education (70 percent). But it seems fairly clear from Tables 1 and 2 that, while the general or liberal goals of higher education are more important to the alumni, they would not be content with a school that did not also provide career training or personality development.

The general strategy of analysis to be followed in this and subsequent chapters is to correlate indices representing the dependent variables under consideration in a given chapter with a number of different sets of variables that might be related to these indices: (1) attributes of the college—quality, size, control (private versus public), type (Catholic, Protestant, university, state college, etc.);

TABLE 2 *Alumni evaluation of goals of faculty and administration at their colleges (Percent)*

	Should have been of	
Aims, intentions, or goals of higher education	*Absolute top importance*	*Absolute top or great importance*
Produce a well-rounded student, that is, one whose physical, social, moral, intellectual, and aesthetic potentialities have all been cultivated	32	80
Assist students to develop objectivity about themselves and their beliefs and hence examine those beliefs critically	24	74
Produce a student who, whatever else may be done to him, has had his intellect cultivated to the maximum	22	60
Train students in methods of scholarship, and/or scientific research, and/or creative endeavor	20	70
Serve as a center for the dissemination of new ideas that will change the society, whether those ideas are in science, literature, the arts, or politics	18	59
Develop the inner character of students so that they can make sound, correct moral choices	18	64
Produce a student who is able to perform his citizenship responsibilities effectively	16	67
Prepare students specifically for useful careers	16	57
Provide the student with skills, attitudes, contacts, and experiences which maximize the likelihood of his occupying a high status in life and a position of leadership in society	12	46
Make sure the student is permanently affected (in mind and spirit) by the great ideas of the great minds of history	11	41
Make a good consumer of the student—a person who is elevated culturally, has good taste, and can make good consumer choices	5	31

(2) experience of the alumni—grades, years in graduate school, quality of graduate school, occupational choice, and present family income; and (3) personal background variables, such as father's education, sex, age, and occasionally, religion.

INDICES OF COLLEGE GOALS Three indices were developed from the responses to the questions discussed in the previous section to facilitate analysis of the variables that influence an alumnus's thinking about the goals of higher education. The indices were labeled *personality development*, *career training*, and *intellectual*, and comprised the following items:

Personality-development index

A goal of my college should have been:

- Produce a well rounded student, that is, one whose physical, social, moral, intellectual, and aesthetic potentialities have all been cultivated.

- Make a good consumer of the student—a person who is elevated culturally, has good taste, and can make good consumer choices.

Career-training index

- College should have trained me for my present job.

- The goal of my college should have been to prepare students specifically for useful careers.

- Purpose of college most important to me personally today is *not* a basic general education and appreciation of ideas.

- College should offer an education that mostly provides general skills and knowledge instead of attempting to provide training for specific jobs. (Neutral, disagree somewhat, disagree strongly)

Intellectual index

A goal of my college should have been:

- Produce a student who, whatever else has been done to him, has had his intellect cultivated to the maximum.

- Assist students to develop objectivity about themselves and their beliefs and hence to examine those beliefs critically.

- Make sure the student is permanently affected (in mind and spirit) by the great ideas of the great minds of history.

- Serve as a center for the dissemination of new ideas that will change the society, whether those ideas are in science, literature, the arts, or politics.

CORRELATES OF COLLEGE GOALS Table 3 presents the coefficients of association (gammas) between the three indices of college goals and the college characteristic and background variables.[1] The composition of the career-training

[1] Gamma has the following properties. If you are asked to predict the rank of a set of responses and are given no further information, you can do no better than guess. If, for every pair of cases that differ with regard to attribute A ($A>B$ or $A<B$), you are told that one member is higher or lower on B than the other, you may be able to use your knowledge of the B-state of the cases to predict their A-state. Gamma is a direct measure of the extent to which knowledge of B *improves* prediction of A. If B is irrelevant, you can still do no better than guess, and gamma will be 0. If the rank of B directly corresponds to that of A, prediction is improved 100 percent, and gamma will be 1.00. If B and A are perfectly inversely related, gamma will be -1.00. For further details, see Goodman and Kruskal (1954).

	Personality-development index	Career-training index	Intellectual index
TABLE 3 Coefficients of association between indices of college goals and background variables (Gamma) — *Background variable*			
College quality	−.20	−.28	.02
College size	−.14	.04	−.06
Control (private)	−.07	−.32	.08
College grades	−.07	−.05	.08
Years in graduate school	−.06	−.13	.11
Graduate school quality	−.20	−.24	.03
Father's education	−.11	−.16	−.01
Sex (male)	−.25	−.22	−.18
Age	.02	.07	−.04
Present family income	−.09	−.14	−.04

index is such that a low score on it indicates a high score on general-education goals. We observe in Table 3 that most of the variables correlate negatively with both the personality-development and the career-training indices. Those who went to high-quality colleges, smaller colleges, and to high-quality graduate schools are the most likely to reject personality-development goals, as are men.[2] Similarly, the graduates of high-quality colleges, of private institutions, and of high-quality graduate schools are also the most likely to reject career-training goals, as are the male members of the sample. In both instances there are moderate negative correlations between both present socioeconomic status (as measured by present family income) and parental socioeconomic status (as measured by father's education) and the values represented by the two indices.

Since the career-training index is merely the opposite end of the continuum represented by a general-education index, one could assert that the graduates of high-quality colleges, of private institutions, of high-quality graduate schools, men, and those with higher socioeconomic background are the ones most likely to endorse the liberal or general goals of higher education.

The most striking findings in Table 3, however, are to be found in the correlations with the intellectual index. Only attendance at graduate school and femininity associate positively with high

[2] College quality is measured by Astin's (1965) *selectivity,* which basically taps an institution's ability to enroll the brighter students it has admitted and corresponds to the average intellectual ability of its freshman class.

scores on this index, and the correlation between the intellectual index and the quality of the institution one has attended is only .02. In other words, the graduates of the high-quality institutions are no more likely than anyone else to see the institution as designed to train students in methods of scholarship or to value the university as a disseminator of new ideas that will change society. This finding, while perhaps not so surprising in light of the low correlations between college quality and cultural activities that we report in the next chapter, is nonetheless a striking one.

Table 4 presents the relationship between college quality and the three indices in percentage form. One can see in the first two columns of the table a regular progression on both the personality-development and the career-training indices from the high-quality colleges to the low. For example, only 12 percent of those in the top schools are in the highest quartile on the personality-development index, while 45 percent of the lowest-quality colleges are in the highest quartile. Only 7 percent of those in the top-quality colleges score in the highest quartile on career training, while 47 percent of those in the low-quality schools score high on that index. On the other hand, there is almost no variation in the column representing the percentages at each quality level that score high on the intellectual index; whether one goes to a "good" school or a "poor" school has no impact on one's evaluation of the strictly intellectual goals of higher education.

The type of college one has attended has, as one might expect on the basis of the previous table, little effect on one's score on the intellectual index but considerable effect on the other two indices (Table 5). Those from state colleges are the most likely

College quality	*Personality-development index*	*Career-training index*	*Intellectual index*
High	12	7	24
	18	23	25
	21	25	23
	28	29	22
	34	40	23
	34	42	24
Low	45	47	30

TABLE 4
Indices of college goals by college quality (Percent in highest quartile)

TABLE 5 *Indices of college goals by type of college attended (Percent)*

Type of college attended	Personality-development index	Career-training index	Intellectual index
University (large public)	26	32	21
University (private)	18	21	24
University (other)	29	43	23
Protestant (low quality)	32	36	20
Protestant (high quality)	25	25	26
State college	39	48	26
Catholic	29	20	28
Liberal arts college	23	7	20

to stress both personality development and career training, while those from private universities and the liberal arts colleges score low on both indices. The graduates of Catholic colleges are somewhat high on the personality-development index and somewhat low on the career-training index, while those who went to Protestant schools of low quality score high on both.

There are substantial variations in the way the occupants of various career positions react to the goals of higher education (Table 6). The personality-development index is most likely to be endorsed by those in the humanities, health professions (other than medicine), and education and least likely to be endorsed by those in biological sciences, engineering, and law. This fact leads one to expect a strong influence of sex, since women are more likely than men to endorse the personality-development index and also more likely than men to occupy the careers that correlate with that index.

The fields in which endorsement of career training instead of general education as a goal of college is highest are "other health," engineering, and education. Alumni in law, medicine, and the humanities are least likely to want career training and therefore most likely to want a general education. That humanists adopt this stance is occasion for no surprise. That doctors and lawyers do so seems to be a different matter. Apparently a major aspect of one's career field is how much practical training in that field is available in college. Future doctors and lawyers typically do not major in their career field. Future engineers and teachers do.

TABLE 6   *Indices of college goals by 1968 career field (Percent)*

1968 career field	Personality-development index	Career-training index	Intellectual index
Physical sciences	21	25	20
Biological sciences	11	18	22
Social sciences	22	20	35
Humanities	30	16	38
Engineering	14	49	7
Medicine	19	14	19
Other health	41	54	28
Education	42	49	29
Business	24	25	17
Law	10	9	26
Other professions	18	24	24

Viewed in this light, the index seems to tap whether a person views college as direct or indirect training for a career in his field.

Finally, those in the social sciences and the humanities are most likely, as one would expect, to be enthusiastic about the intellectual goals of higher education, while those in engineering and business are the least likely to support these goals.

To summarize this chapter thus far, there seem to be three important dimensions of higher education values—development of a well-rounded personality, training for a career, and development of intellectual skills, with career training representing the reverse side of the coin on which is to be found a general-education dimension. Women score highest both on the personality-development and on the intellectual indices, but also score highest on the career-training index, which means that women are more likely to endorse intellectual goals than men but less likely to endorse general goals. Students from high-quality undergraduate or graduate institutions are more inclined to be against both personality development and career training but are no more likely than anyone else to see the goals of higher education as intellectual.

Multiple regression techniques were used to analyze the variance on the three goals-of-education indices: 8 percent of the variance on the personality-development index was explained, a respectable 18 percent on the career-training index, and only 6 percent of the variance on the intellectual index. The most powerful explanatory variables with regard to the personality-development index were sex, father's education, and the quality of the college one attended. The strongest explanatory variables in the model dealing with the career-training index were, again, sex, father's education, and college quality. Sex and years in graduate school were the only strong explanatory variables in the model dealing with the intellectual index. Women, then, are more likely to endorse intellectual goals and less likely to endorse general goals but are also more likely to endorse career-training and personality-development goals for higher education. Those from well-educated family backgrounds are less likely to be concerned about personality development and career training and hence more concerned about general education, and those who have gone to graduate school, understandably enough, are somewhat more concerned about intellectual goals precisely because graduate training presumably requires the skills that the intellectual index represents.

Our three multiple regression models, therefore, lead us to conclude that sex persists in being the strongest predictor of alumni values with regard to goals of higher education. Men stress general-education goals; women stress career training and personality development as goals. Those who attended high-quality schools are more likely to endorse general goals of higher education (as opposed to career-training goals) and less likely to emphasize personality-development goals. However, there is little difference between the graduates of high- and low-quality institutions in the scores on the intellectual index. Two career fields, engineering and education, also help to explain the variance in the indices, with engineers emphasizing career training and deemphasizing both intellectualism and personality development, while those in education strongly emphasize career training as a goal.

It is possible to fit the findings reported in this chapter into a fairly neat explanatory scheme. Men emphasize general as opposed to career education because in many of the professions they choose there is, at the present time, little career preparation possible during one's undergraduate years. Women stress well-rounded personality development both because this index represents a complex of qualities that are thought to be important in the role of a wife and mother and because in the careers that women choose, education and "other health" in particular, the ability to deal with people is extremely important. The intellectual goals are popular with the social scientists and the humanists because these goals represent the skills that are part of their stock-in-trade. Career training is popular with engineers, while the other two goals are relatively unpopular with them, because engineering colleges provide rather precise career training for their students and because neither the well-rounded personality nor the specific intellectual skills of the scholar are required for the professional engineer. In other words, one's values with regard to higher education are shaped very much by what one's life is. If one is a doctor or a lawyer or even a businessman, one values training as a "generalist." If one is a housewife, a teacher, a nurse, or a humanist, one values the well-rounded personality. If one is an engineer or a teacher, one values career training. And if one is a social scientist or a humanist, one values those intellectual skills that are important in one's discipline.

All of which is to suggest that the alumni emphasize as important goals of higher education precisely those attributes that they find important in their own particular life position. From this point of view, the traditional distinction between the general and vocational dimensions of education seems rather irrelevant. The goals of higher education that are important to our alumni are those goals which seem most functional for their own present life situations. Those who are more likely to emphasize general education are those who need the generalist skills in their present life role; those who emphasize the well-rounded personality need the well-rounded personality in their life role; and those who emphasize intellectual skills need intellectual skills in their life role. Finally, those who emphasize career training are those for whom higher education has traditionally been able to provide highly specific "how-to-do-it" courses.

SUMMARY AND CONCLUSION The most striking finding in the present chapter is that the life role seems to be the principal available explanation for the variance in the alumni's choice of appropriate goals for higher education. Career training is endorsed by those who presently find that career training was helpful to them; personality development is emphasized especially by those who need interpersonal skills in their present life situation; intellectual skills are emphasized by those whose profession demands the tools of the scholar; and general preparation is stressed by those whose professional development occurs more in graduate school than in undergraduate school. Thus, the traditional distinction between general and vocational education does not seem to be a valid one for the 1961 graduates. The alumni, of course, are more sympathetically disposed toward general or intellectual goals than they are toward career-training goals for higher education, and as we shall see later, their ideas about the reform of higher education are strongly generalist, if not to say humanist. But the critical conclusion to be derived from this chapter is that if general or intellectual or liberal goals of higher education are more important to the alumni, it is primarily because their present life role seems to demand the skills that general or liberal or intellectual education provides. Furthermore, while they are somewhat less likely to endorse specific vocational training, it is clear that they do not reject vocational education but are rather more likely to think of it more broadly than do the professional educators. The M.D. who stresses general education as a goal; the sociologist who stresses intellectual development; and the housewife, the teacher, or the nurse who stresses the well-rounded personality—all have very much in mind the specific occupational challenges that they are presently experiencing as the third decade of their life draws to an end.

The principal findings reported in this chapter are as follows:

1   The general or liberal goals of higher education are more popular with the alumni than the vocational goals (but the vocational goals are by no means rejected).

2   A cluster of goals that could be called intellectual and that does not correlate with general-education goals relates strongly only to sex (women are more intellectual) and is completely unaffected by quality of college attended.

3   Those who went to high-quality colleges, smaller colleges, and high-quality graduate schools are the most likely to reject personality-development goals, as are men.

4   The graduates of high-quality colleges, of private institutions, and of high-quality graduate schools, and also men are the most likely to reject career training and to endorse general education.

5   Life role is closely related to the alumni's choice of goals for higher education: career training is endorsed by those who find career training is helpful to them in their life role; personality development is emphasized by those who need interpersonal skills in their present life situation; intellectual skills are emphasized by those whose profession demands the tools of the scholar; and general preparation is stressed by those whose professional training occurs more in graduate school than in college.

3. College and Culture

Although there are some educators who will argue that the traditional liberal goals of higher education are no longer appropriate at a time of mass higher education, there still is a fairly wide consensus in American higher education—symbolically represented by the college catalog—that the training of the "educated man" is one of the major purposes of higher education. Exactly what constitutes an educated man is still a matter for much debate, and social science can make no pretense of being able to measure all the nuances of the cultivated mind as described, for example, by John Henry Newman in *Idea of a University* (1960 ed.). All the social scientist can do is ask rather gross questions to provide some kind of rough information about the behavior of college graduates. It is, of course, possible for someone to read very little; to ignore music, drama, museums, and other cultural concerns; and still to be profoundly affected by the western intellectual, cultural tradition and to have a sensitive, balanced mind and clear powers of expression. Yet one must assume that the number of people who would fit into such a category is relatively small and that reading and cultural behaviors are at least rough indicators of the achievement of the goals of a liberal education. In the context of such an assumption, the findings of the present chapter are presented.

It is impossible, without being able to make comparisons with those who do not go to college—comparisons in which all other background variables are held constant—to define precisely the impact of higher education on the cultural behavior of its graduates. Presumably our alumni read more and are more interested in the arts than their age peers who did not attend college, but whether this is the effect of their college education or merely of their social class background and raw intellectual ability is beyond the scope of our present efforts. We can, however, ask whether the graduates of the better colleges are more likely to engage in cultural activities, for if higher education does produce people who are more likely to read or to be interested in the arts, then presumably the better the college, the more the involvement would be. If such a phenomenon were to be observed, of course one would have to filter out the background variables that might be responsible for the apparent success of the better institutions. Perhaps Harvard graduates read more because they read more before they went to Harvard. On the other hand, if there is only a small relationship between cultural activities and the quality of one's higher educational institution, there is some reason to suspect that higher education has relatively little effect on behavior patterns that, in some rough way, might measure activity appropriate for the educated man.

PARTICIPA-
TION IN
CULTURAL
ACTIVITIES

Table 7 summarizes the responses of the 1961 graduates regarding their participation in cultural activities. One must be very cautious in interpreting these percentages, since the survey researcher deliberately designs his category response pattern to provide a distribution of responses across the entire pattern. A large majority of the alumni claim to read serious fiction and nonfiction at least "occasionally" and to listen to classical music at least "occasionally," while smaller majorities claim at least "occasionally" to attend concerts, to attend plays, or to visit museums

TABLE 7
Cultural
activities of
1961 alumni
(Percent)

Cultural activity	I do this	
	Frequently	*Frequently or occasionally*
Read (not necessarily finish) a nonfiction book	39	81
Read (not necessarily finish) a work of "serious fiction"	26	66
Read poetry	6	26
Listen to classical or serious music	32	69
Go to concerts	8	41
Go to plays	13	57
Go to museums or art galleries	11	56
Travel abroad	6	21

and art galleries. Only a minority, however, claim to go to concerts, and but one-quarter claim to read poetry at least "occasionally." Much smaller groups are willing to claim that they read "frequently," and with the exception of the fans of serious music (one-third of the respondents claim to listen to it "frequently"), only very small groups report that they "frequently" engage in other cultural activities.

In the absence of data about the reading habits and interest in the arts of the total American population of the same age group as our respondents, it is impossible to say whether the levels of activity reported by our respondents represent any very notable difference between those young people who attended college and those who did not. Presumably, however, there would be some differences. While the critical question in this chapter is not the tabulations but the relationships between behavior and background variables, one is still forced to note that the percentages reported in Table 7 are not likely to produce much consolation for those educators who value the traditional liberal goals of higher education. Such educators will be at least partially consoled by the figures in Table 8, which indicate that one-third of the 1961 alumni own 300 or more books, though they may be somewhat taken aback by the thought that almost two-fifths own less than 150 books. (This is equivalent, we find, to the contents of a standard four-shelf bookcase.)

ATTITUDES ON SCIENCE AND TECHNOLOGY

Although no information is available for comparative purposes on reading and interest in the arts among the general population, comparative data have been obtained on another set of indicators that might be presumed to measure roughly the liberal goals of higher education. One would presume that the educated man has confidence in science, is not threatened by the changing pace of the world, and does not feel a sense of alienation and anomie vis-à-vis

TABLE 8
Number of books owned by 1961 alumni

Number of books	Percent
Under 150	38
150–299	29
300 or more	33
TOTAL	100

his society. In Table 9 we observe that college alumni are considerably less likely to feel that science is causing the world to change too fast and that the "experts" have replaced "ordinary" people in positions of social control. More than one-half of the general population think that science is causing the world to change too fast, whereas only one-quarter of the alumni would agree with such a proposition. And almost three-quarters of the general population think that the experts have too much power, while only about two-fifths of the alumni would assent to such an idea. It is, nonetheless, interesting to note that about two-fifths of the alumni *do* have suspicions of the experts and that one-quarter of them *are* restless about the pace of change induced by science. Given the complexities of American society and the difficulty in changing human attitudes, one might conclude that educators ought to be happy that as many as three-quarters of the respondents *do not* think that the world is changing too fast and that three-fifths *do not* resent the power of the experts.

TABLE 9 **Attitudes on science and technology for alumni and for the general population (Percent agree strongly or somewhat)**

Attitude	Alumni	General population
Scientific research is causing the world to change too fast	26	54
Because the experts have so much power in our society, ordinary people don't have much of a say in things	38	72

INDICES OF CULTURAL ACTIVITIES The critical question to which this chapter addresses itself is whether the kind of college a young person attended or the experiences he had in college correlate with his cultural activities.

Two indices were prepared to describe cultural activities—the *serious-reading* index and the *interest-in-the-arts* index. These include the following items:

Serious-reading index
- Read (not necessarily finish) a nonfiction book
- Read (not necessarily finish) a work of "serious fiction"
- Read poetry
- Number of books owned

Interest-in-the-arts index
- Listen to classical or serious music

- Go to concerts

- Go to plays

- Go to museums or art galleries

It should be remembered, with all these indices, that they are nothing more than patterns of response to a group of questions and that even though we give them a nominative label, the label merely describes the pattern of response and, not necessarily with any degree of precision, the reality normally described by the same word.

CORRELATES OF CULTURAL ACTIVITIES Table 10 indicates that there is relatively little relationship between the quality of college a young person attended and his cultural activities. While there is a gamma of .14 between interest in the arts and the quality of the college, the other gammas are inconsequential, and even the .14 association between college quality and interest in the arts is hardly very exciting. The strongest predictor of whether people read or are interested in the arts is their sex. As one might expect, women are much more likely to participate in cultural activities than are men (a gamma of —.27 for interest in the arts and —.30 for serious reading). In addition to sex, one's college grades, the number of years one has spent in graduate school, and the quality of graduate school attended all demonstrate an association with cultural activities of about .2 (save graduate

TABLE 10
Coefficients of association between indices of cultural activities and background variables (Gamma)

Background variable	Interest-in-the-arts index	Serious-reading index
College quality	.14	.08
College size	—.01	—.02
Control (private)	.05	.05
College grades	.17	.21
Years in graduate school	.18	.20
Graduate school quality	.18	.09
Father's education	.13	.11
Sex (male)	—.27	—.30
Age	—.12	—.09
Present family income	.10	.07

TABLE 11
*Indices of
cultural
activities by
type of college
attended
(Percent in
highest
quartile)*

Type of college attended	Interest-in-the-arts index	Serious-reading index
University (large public)	22	22
University (private)	26	26
University (other)	23	21
Protestant (low quality)	14	17
Protestant (high quality)	28	25
State college	20	23
Catholic	17	24
Liberal arts college	30	23

school quality and reading, where the association drops to .09). It is worth noting that quality of institution, whether graduate or undergraduate, is considerably less likely to be associated with reading behavior than with interest in the arts; in the former instance the associations with college quality are less than .1. One is forced to conclude, therefore, that the quality of the higher educational institution which one attends has little relationship with the amount of serious reading one does after graduation.[1]

The conclusion is reinforced by the data presented in Table 11. There is little relationship between the *type* of college one has attended and one's reading behavior. Only those from Protestant colleges of low quality deviate much below 25 percent on reading behavior. On the index measuring interest in the arts, there is somewhat more variation, with the graduates of the liberal arts colleges measuring somewhat over the 25 percent level and the graduates of Catholic and "low-quality" Protestant colleges measuring somewhat under it. The type of college one attends, therefore, does not affect one's reading very much, but may affect slightly one's inclination to listen to music, attend concerts, or visit museums.

While the gamma coefficient is an efficient way of measuring relationships, it does not provide the richness of detail offered

---

[1] This is a conclusion that ought to be profoundly disturbing to American educators.

by the multivariate table. Since the issue of the relationship between college quality and interest in the arts and reading behavior of the alumni is of some importance, it is worthwhile to inspect the tables represented by gamma coefficients between college quality and cultural activities. In Table 12 there is a spread of but 8 percentage points between the proportion high on the serious-reading index from the highest-quality colleges and the proportion high on the serious-reading index from the very lowest-quality colleges; 30 percent of those from the best colleges in the country are in the highest quartile of reading behavior, compared with 22 percent of those from the poorest colleges. The differences are somewhat more impressive on the interest-in-the-arts index, with 32 percent of those from the top colleges and only 14 percent of those from the poorest colleges being in the highest quartile. One cannot escape the conclusion that the quality of education does influence to some extent the alumni's position on measures of interest in the arts, but does not affect in any notable fashion their position on measures of serious-reading behavior.

However, there is, as one might expect, a strong relationship between career choice and cultural activities (Table 13). Those who have chosen careers in the humanities are the most likely to score high on our indices, while those in engineering and business are the least likely to be in the top quartile of cultural activities. Generally speaking, one can say that those in the arts and sciences (with the exception of the physical sciences) are likely to score high, while those in the professions (with the exception of medicine) are likely to score low. Our data do not enable us

	Interest-in-the-arts index	Serious-reading index
TABLE 12 *Indices of cultural activities by college quality (Percent in highest quartile)* *College quality*		
High	32	30
	24	23
	26	22
	24	24
	15	18
	20	22
Low	14	22

	Interest-in-the-arts index	Serious-reading index
TABLE 13 *Indices of cultural activities by 1968 career field (Percent in highest quartile)* 1968 career field		
Physical sciences	22	17
Biological sciences	33	38
Social sciences	32	26
Humanities	44	52
Engineering	11	10
Medicine	32	26
Other health	24	27
Education	20	26
Business	14	11
Law	23	18
Other professions	22	25

to answer the question of whether people choose certain careers because they have cultural interests or whether their careers lead them to have broader cultural interests. Presumably, the influence runs in both directions.

To summarize our findings thus far, sex and career choice seem to have the strongest impact on reading and interest in the arts, while the quality of school (undergraduate and graduate) influences interest in the arts somewhat but reading behavior only marginally.

A multiple regression analysis was done on the two indices of cultural activities, using the background, career, and college-type variables with which we have been working. Only relatively small amounts of the variance were explained by these models — 12 percent of the variance on the interest-in-the-arts index and a similar percentage of the variance on the serious-reading index. Given the small amount of variance explained, we shall merely summarize the results and not present the complete data. The principal explanatory variables in the interest-in-the-arts index were sex (4 percent of the variance) and a choice of a career in the humanities (2 percent of the variance). The strongest explanatory variables in the model dealing with the serious-reading index were college grades (3 percent of the variance), career choice in the humanities (1 percent of the variance), and a career choice in any other career but business (1 percent of the variance). In both models, college quality explained less than 1 percent of the variance. In other words, when family background variables were held constant, the variation in cultural activities among the June, 1961 alumni seven years after graduation that could be explained by the quality of the college they attended was less than 1 percent. Despite the fact that our measures on serious reading and interest in the arts are far from perfect, it still seems safe to conclude that the relationship which college quality has with reading and interest in the arts is trivial, even if we are prepared to grant that it is very difficult for a college—even a high-quality college—to affect what has already been shaped by home and family background. Relatively little more has been achieved in modifying reading and interest in the arts by the best colleges in the country than has been done by the poorest colleges.

A very striking phenomenon to be observed in Table 14 is that women from the lowest-quality colleges are almost as likely to report that they listen "frequently" to serious music (37 percent) as are men from the highest-quality colleges (40 percent). Similarly, women from the lowest-quality colleges are as likely to report "frequently" reading serious fiction (29 percent) as are men from the highest-quality colleges (27 percent). Furthermore, for men, college quality does seem to have some impact on both their reading serious fiction and their listening to serious music. The difference between the highest- and lowest-quality colleges is 24 percentage points on the music item and 15 percentage points on the reading item. For women, the quality of college has a similar impact on listening to music, but there is little in the way of a

	Frequently listen to serious music		Frequently read serious fiction	
College quality	Men	Women	Men	Women
High	40	57	27	35
	33	40	19	42
	35	43	22	37
	32	38	16	44
	19	32	16	29
	25	34	15	35
Low	16	37	12	29

TABLE 14 *Cultural activities by sex and college quality (Percent)*

clear relationship between college quality and reading serious fiction.

We are thus in a position to modify somewhat the statement made previously about the relationship between these indices and college quality. Table 14 enables us to say that at least as far as reading serious fiction is concerned, college quality does have some impact on the male population, though not much on the female population. Those male alumni who went to better colleges are more likely to read serious fiction than those who did not. Nevertheless, the major point in this table is that sex is a far stronger predictor of serious reading and interest in serious music than is college quality.

In discussing with educators the rather startling lack of relationship between school quality and reading, the author of this chapter encountered two reactions. The first was simply to dismiss survey research as an inadequate tool for measuring literary interests. The second was to accept the finding and then to explain it away either, as one educator did, by saying that higher education had other roles besides the production of people who read, or by arguing, as yet another educator put it, that graduates of low-quality schools obviously were striving very hard to keep up with the reading habits of the graduates of high-quality schools. One is somewhat at a loss on how to respond to such argumentation. Obviously, survey research is filled with limitations and imperfections. Whether people read as much as they say they read may be problematic. Nevertheless, even the fact that the graduates of high-quality schools fail to *report* much more reading than do the graduates of low-quality schools is a striking commentary on American higher education. Furthermore, while the education of people who read may not be the only goal of higher education, one scarcely knows what to say to an educator who argues that it is not an important goal.

Finally, one could just as easily postulate the phenomenon in which the graduates of high-quality schools tried to keep their reading levels low so as not to embarrass the graduates of poorer schools as one could postulate a mysterious sort of need for achievement that would impel the graduates of poorer schools to compete successfully in reading behavior with the graduates of elite institutions. One concludes that the educators with whom the findings were discussed simply could not bring themselves to admit that a very low association between quality in educational institutions and alumni reading behavior was a serious possibility. Yet our data incline us to accept the finding at its face value, however unpleasant it may be for American higher education: *How much you read does not seem to be influenced by the quality of the college you attended.*

The items that were designed to measure respondents' reactions to power and technology were combined into an "antiexperts" index containing the following items:

- Scientific research is causing the world to change too fast.

- Because the experts have so much power in our society, ordinary people don't have much of a say in things.

- It's not enough to be a college graduate these days, you have to graduate from a good college to get a job worth having.

The relationship of background variables to the antiexperts index is analyzed in Tables 15, 16, and 17. There is a moderate negative association between the antiexperts index and college quality, college size, college grades, father's education, and sex (male). Those who went to lower-quality colleges and smaller colleges, those who got lower grades, women, and those with a relatively low socioeconomic status (as measured by father's education) are more likely to be suspicious of science and technology than their counterparts (Table 15). Similarly, those who went to "low-quality" Protestant colleges, state colleges, and "other" universities are most likely to be in the highest quartile of the antiexperts index (Table 16). Among the career fields, those whose professional choices inclined them to the humanities and to educa-

TABLE 15
Coefficients of association between antiexperts index and background variables

Background variable	Gamma
College quality	—.09
College size	—.08
Control (private)	—.01
College grades	—.08
Years in graduate school	—.01
Father's education	—.08
Sex (male)	—.08

TABLE 16 Antiexperts index by type of college attended	
Type of college attended	Percent in highest quartile
University (large public)	18
University (private)	17
University (other)	26
Protestant (low quality)	27
Protestant (high quality)	19
State college	27
Catholic	23
Liberal arts college	19

TABLE 17 Antiexperts index by 1968 career field	
1968 career field	Percent in highest quartile
Physical sciences	15
Biological sciences	21
Social sciences	13
Humanities	30
Engineering	20
Medicine	14
Other health	22
Education	27
Business	18
Law	16
Other professions	22

tion are the ones most likely to object to the power of the expert (Table 17). The antiexperts index, then, seems in some ways to be the reverse of the reading and interest-in-the-arts indices (although women are likely to score positively on all three). The important point to be made, however, is that just as the graduates of high-quality colleges are only very slightly more likely to read, so are they only slightly more likely to reject opinions expressing suspicion of science and technology.

SUMMARY   In this chapter we have considered the cultural activity of the June, 1961 alumni and their attitudes toward science and technology. The principal findings reported are as follows:

1 There is a moderate relationship (gamma = .14) between college quality and interest in the arts, a relationship that is reduced when sex, parental socioeconomic status (as represented by father's education), and religion are held constant.

2 The relationship between college quality and reading is minimal.

3 Sex is by far the strongest predictor of both reading and interest in the arts, with women being far more likely than men to engage in both.

4 The graduates of high-quality institutions are only slightly more in sympathy with technology than the graduates of lower-quality institutions.

4. Memories of Alma Mater

One could summarize the reactions of the June, 1961 alumni to the colleges in which they received their undergraduate training by saying that the colleges are similar to Willy Loman — they are liked, but not well liked. Table 18 compares the reactions of the alumni at the time of graduation with their reactions in 1968. Both those who have a strong attachment to their college and those who have mixed feelings have declined in number, while those who like their college but do not have strong feelings have now risen to almost three-fifths of the population. It could be that experience in the postgraduate world has made some alumni more realistic about their college, or it could be that the mere passing of time has moderated strong reactions, whether they be positive or negative. In either case, their nostalgia for their alma mater does not seem to be overwhelming.

The decline of strong positive feelings toward the college that the respondents attended can also be observed in Table 19. While most alumni one year after graduation were ready to say that teaching, course offerings, facilities, fellow students, and faculty were at least "good," there was an erosion over time of several percentage points on each item.

In Table 20 we note that the majority of the alumni were willing to reject most of the standard criticisms of student life, with rejection of intenseness of grade pressure being the only item to fall well below the 50-50 level. But the majority did not think that the rules were too restrictive, or that there was no chance to do anything of service to the community, or that there was no opportunity to understand society or self, or that the school was not intellectually stimulating. On the other hand, at least two-fifths of the respondents were willing to concede at least some truth to each of these charges.

TABLE 18
**Emotional
feeling about
college or
university from
which bachelor's
degree was
obtained, 1961
and 1968
(Percent)**

Emotional feelings about college or university	1961	1968
I have a very strong attachment to it	32	27
I like it, but my feelings are not strong	44	59
Mixed feelings	18	11
I don't like it much, but my feelings are not strong	4	3
I thoroughly dislike it	2	1

TABLE 19   *Alumni evaluation of undergraduate college or university, 1962 and 1968 (Percent)*

Aspects of undergraduate college or university	1962		1968	
	Excellent	Excellent or good	Excellent	Excellent or good
Caliber of classroom teaching	23	77	18	71
Curriculum and course offerings	30	75	22	69
Facilities and opportunities for research (including library)	27	54	24	56
Student housing	22	55	16	49
Caliber of the students	22	67	20	66
Knowledge and professional standing of the faculty	42	86	29	76
Personal contacts with faculty	–	–	15	46

TABLE 20
**Alumni
reactions to
criticisms of
colleges
(Percent)**

Criticisms of college attended	Not true at all
There was no sense of community or chance for students to participate	49
The rules were too restrictive	56
There was no chance to do anything of service to the community	53
There was no opportunity to understand society or myself	62
It was not intellectually stimulating	59
The pressure for grades was too intense	36

About one-third of the alumni thought that their college prepared them very well for graduate or professional school, and seven-eighths said that it prepared them at least moderately well (Table 21). Twenty-seven percent found that their college prepared them very well for their job; 42 percent said the same of graduate or professional school preparation for jobs. Thus, we find in Table 21 the same moderate reaction as prevails toward other aspects of one's college.

In Table 22 we discover how the alumni rate their college on its performance in terms of the goals the alumni have established as being important. The single most impressive phenomenon to be observed in this table is that only on two items—training for their present job and the forming of friendships—is a greater proportion of the alumni willing to say that the college actually affected them greatly or somewhat than the proportion saying that they think the college should have affected them. The gap between expectation and performance is larger in matters such as "ability to think and express oneself," "broad knowledge of arts and sciences," "tolerance for people and ideas," and "formulation of values and goals of life" than it is for the career-training and personality variables. Those goals that the alumni think are most important are also the ones for which there seems to be the greatest gap between expectation and performance. Nevertheless, on all but two items ("preparation for marriage" and "helping others") the majority of the

		Very or moderately well
Question	*Very well*	
*How well do you think your undergraduate college prepared you for graduate or professional school?**	31	87
How well would you say each of the following prepared you for the job you currently hold?		
General college training	27	86
Major program	29	78
*Graduate or professional school**	42	87

TABLE 21
College as a preparation for graduate or professional school and job (Percent)

*Asked only of those who went to graduate or professional school.

TABLE 22 *Percent responding to the questions: "Which of the following do you think your college should have given you?" and "Whether or not you think you should have gotten each of these things, please rate the extent to which your college affected you in each of these ways"*

Item	I think my college should have	My college actually affected me	
		Greatly	Greatly or somewhat
Developed my abilities to think and express myself	98	41	87
Given me a broad knowledge of the arts and sciences	90	35	77
Expanded my tolerance for people and ideas	90	34	75
Helped me to learn how to make my own decisions	81	20	73
Helped me to formulate the values and goals of my life	80	20	64
Prepared me to get ahead in the world	70	18	66
Helped me to learn how to get along with others	69	23	68
Trained me for my present job	65	34	67
Helped me to learn ways of helping people	60	10	43
Helped me to form valuable and lasting friendships	54	25	57
Helped prepare me for marriage and family	39	7	30

alumni are willing to say that their college actually affected them at least "somewhat."

The findings in Table 23 complement those reported in Table 22. However, the differences between expectation and performance are made even clearer. One need merely look down the column headed "Absolute top importance" to see that in no instance do as many alumni think that the faculty and administration actually *had* the given goals as the proportion of alumni that think the faculty and administration *should have had* such goals. Furthermore, the differences between expectation and performance are highest at the top half of the table, with at least twice as many (and on some items three times as many) alumni saying that a given item *should have been* of "absolute top importance" to faculty and administration as are willing to say that a particular item *was* of "absolute top importance." It does not seem to be an exaggeration to suggest that American higher education has a serious problem with its graduates when 32 percent say that the faculty and administration *should have* considered the production of the well-rounded student of "absolute top importance," while only 14 percent say that, in fact, it *was* of "absolute top importance." Similarly, educators can hardly rest content with the knowledge that 24 percent of the alumni claim that the development of objectivity *should have been* of "absolute top importance" to faculty and administrators, but only 7 percent say that they thought it actually *was* of "absolute top importance."

Nor do the alumni think that college had a very powerful influence on their reading habits and interest in the arts (Table 24). Although on most items the majority are willing to concede that their college had at least "moderate" influence on their cultural behavior, no more than one-fifth see their college's influence as "great." One can only conclude that Table 24 is another indication of what can at best be called a moderate level of satisfaction with the higher educational experience.

To summarize the preliminary findings stated in this chapter, the June, 1961 alumni are moderately attached to their colleges, though less so than they were at the time of graduation. A majority reject most of the criticisms aimed at quality of student life, but a substantial minority endorse these criticisms. Finally, a comparison between what the alumni think their college should have done and what it actually did accomplish suggests a fair amount of dissatisfaction with the higher educational experience. It must be emphasized, however, that nothing reported thus far indicates that dissatisfaction is strongly felt by a large proportion of the graduates, much less that they are radically disenchanted with the American higher educational enterprise.

MEASURES OF ATTITUDES TOWARD COLLEGE

In the analytical section of this chapter we shall use four dependent variables: emotional attachment to one's college, the desirability of sending one's children to one's alma mater, and scores on two indices—one, an index based on Table 19 and measuring the *perceived quality of alma mater,* and the other based on Table 20 and measuring the *criticism of student life* at the school. The two indices contain the following items:

Perceived-quality-of-alma-mater index

Rating of the following aspects of undergraduate college:

- Caliber of classroom teaching
- Curriculum and course offerings
- Facilities and opportunities for research (including library)

Aims, intentions, or goals of higher education

Produce a well-rounded student, that is, one whose physical, social, moral, intellectual, and aesthetic potentialities have all been cultivated

Assist students to develop objectivity about themselves and their beliefs and hence examine those beliefs critically

Produce a student who, whatever else may be done to him, has had his intellect cultivated to the maximum

Train students in methods of scholarship, and/or scientific research, and/or creative endeavor

Serve as a center for the dissemination of new ideas that will change the society, whether those ideas are in science, literature, the arts, or politics

Develop the inner character of students so that they can make sound, correct moral choices

Produce a student who is able to perform his citizenship responsibilities effectively

Prepare students specifically for useful careers

Provide the student with skills, attitudes, contacts, and experiences which maximize the likelihood of his occupying a high status in life and a position of leadership in society

Make sure the student is permanently affected (in mind and spirit) by the great ideas of the great minds of history

Make a good consumer of the student—a person who is elevated culturally, has good taste, and can make good consumer choices

- Caliber of the students
- Knowledge and professional standing of the faculty

Criticisms of college:

- It was not intellectually stimulating. (Not at all true.)

Criticism-of-student-life index

Criticisms of college attended:

- There was no sense of community or chance for students to participate.
- There was no chance to do anything of service to the community.
- There was no opportunity to understand society or myself.

Absolute top importance		Absolute top or great importance	
Should have been	Was	Should have been	Was
32	14	80	50
24	7	74	37
22	6	60	32
20	9	70	42
18	6	59	27
18	10	64	37
16	6	67	37
16	14	57	54
12	5	46	30
11	4	41	24
5	2	31	19

Before we proceed with this analysis, we should note that there is a fairly strong gamma coefficient (.42) between the quality of the college as perceived by the alumni and the index of academic quality used in this report; alumni are in reasonably good agreement with Astin's (1965) estimation of college quality. Two percent of the alumni think it would be "very desirable" to send their children to their own school and 16 percent more think it would be at least "somewhat desirable."

CORRELATES OF ATTITUDES TOWARD COLLEGE In Table 25 we turn to the question of the relationship between various background variables and attitudes toward the college attended. Even granted the fairly low level of gamma coefficients normally uncovered in survey research of the sort described in this

TABLE 24
Alumni perception of influence of college on cultural activities (Percent)

Cultural activity	College was of	
	Great influence	Great or moderate influence
Read (not necessarily finish) a nonfiction book	20	73
Read (not necessarily finish) a work of "serious fiction"	14	66
Read poetry	11	48
Listen to classical or serious music	14	52
Go to concerts	10	48
Go to plays	11	55
Go to museums or art galleries	10	53
Travel abroad	5	25

TABLE 25 **Coefficients of association between attitudes toward college attended and background variables (Gamma)**

Background variable	Emotional attachment	Desirable to send children to alma mater	Criticism index	Perceived-quality index
College quality	.12	.11	−.01	.42
College size	.00	−.01	.07	.13
Control (private)	.04	.09	−.04	.12
College grades	−.01	−.07	−.01	.00
Years in graduate school	.03	.05	.01	.01
Graduate school quality	.11	.02	−.07	.25
Father's education	.04	.01	−.04	.14
Sex (male)	−.02	.04	.00	−.05
Age	−.06	−.12	−.01	−.07
Present family income	.07	.00	−.03	.16

report, the very low gammas in Table 25 are surprising. Only two background variables associate with emotional attachment at a level above .1—college quality (.12) and graduate school quality (.11). There is a .11 correlation between college quality and inclination to send one's own children to one's alma mater, and a .12 correlation between such inclination and youth. There are no meaningful relationships of any sort between criticism of the school and any of the background variables. And while there are some associations between the background variables and the perceived quality of the college, none of these is higher than .2, save the .25 between perceived quality of the college and graduate school quality and the .42 already reported between objective and perceived college quality. Positive associations between perceived quality and size of the college, private control, father's education, and present family income are at best very moderate.

One supposes that it is not too surprising that variables such as sex, family socioeconomic background, and age would only correlate moderately, if at all, with attitudes toward one's educational institution. It is somewhat surprising, however, that the size of the college, its control, and even its actual quality should associate at such a very low level with emotional attachment or the inclination to send one's own children to the same institution.

Table 26, which provides data on the relationship between the dependent variables and the kind of college one attended, however, provides some more interesting findings. Those who went to "other" universities, state colleges, and Catholic colleges are more likely to score high on the criticism index and those who went to liberal arts colleges are likely to score lower than average on the index. Precisely the same groups—that is, the graduates of "other" universities, state colleges, and Catholic colleges—also score rather

TABLE 26 *Attitudes toward college attended, by type of college attended*

	Percent in highest quartile		Percent	
Type of college attended	Criticism index	Perceived-quality index	Strong attachment to college	Desirable to send children to alma mater
University (large public)	29	29	29	18
University (private)	27	52	33	22
University (other)	36	22	20	12
Protestant (low quality)	23	12	26	19
Protestant (high quality)	20	24	23	16
State college	31	9	16	12
Catholic	35	14	35	29
Liberal arts college	16	53	39	28

low in their evaluation of the academic quality of the college, though they are joined in this somewhat negative evaluation of their alma mater by the graduates of the "low-quality" Protestant colleges. Further, the graduates of the private universities and liberal arts colleges are twice as likely as the typical American alumnus to score in the highest quartile on the perceived-quality index.

The third column of Table 26 provides only one surprise. As expected, the graduates of the private universities and the liberal arts colleges are the ones most likely to be strongly attached. They perceive the quality of their college as high and they score relatively low on the criticism index; one would expect them to be strongly attached to their alma mater. Nevertheless, the graduates of Catholic colleges, who score high on the criticism index and low on the perceived-quality index, are only a little less likely than the graduates of liberal arts colleges to be strongly attached to their colleges. Furthermore, they are more likely than the graduates of any other kind of institution to say that it would be desirable to send their children to their own alma mater. One concludes, therefore, that something about the Catholic college experience offsets the rather low opinion graduates of Catholic colleges have of the schools' academic quality and of the organization and regulation of student life.

Both the actual quality of a college, as measured by Astin's (1965) index of quality, and the perceived quality, as measured by the alumni's perception of the excellence of various features of their institution, predict emotional attachment to the college and a desire to send one's children to one's alma mater. It is legitimate to wonder whether objective quality or subjective perception of quality has the stronger influence. Table 27 leaves little doubt about the conclusion when subjective perception of the quality of the school is held constant. Its objective quality — at least as measured by Astin's index — has little or no effect on either emotional attachment to the college or inclination to send one's children to the same school. Evaluation, then, of one's higher educational experience has a powerful subjective component.

If the kind of school attended does seem to have some impact on the reaction of the alumni, one may wonder whether the kind of career they have chosen has a similar effect. Doctors and lawyers are much more likely to perceive their schools as of high quality because, in all likelihood, they attended high-quality schools (Table

TABLE 27
Attitudes toward college attended, by college quality (Astin index) and perceived quality of college (Percent)

College quality (Astin index)	Perceived quality of college			
	High			Low
	Strong attachment to college			
High	54 (276)	38 (55)	* (7)	* (2)
	51 (320)	38 (206)	30 (61)	10 (60)
	37 (360)	29 (396)	15 (214)	7 (196)
	40 (551)	24 (877)	27 (538)	8 (386)
	56 (167)	34 (290)	26 (279)	12 (491)
	53 (127)	24 (360)	20 (301)	9 (494)
Low	49 (53)	29 (155)	24 (163)	12 (327)
	Desirable to send children to alma mater			
High	36 (273)	18 (50)	* (7)	* (2)
	33 (321)	27 (203)	21 (62)	5 (57)
	29 (354)	18 (392)	11 (212)	10 (196)
	22 (545)	22 (869)	10 (545)	6 (385)
	39 (165)	28 (294)	16 (280)	10 (484)
	30 (127)	18 (357)	16 (314)	14 (494)
Low	22 (50)	17 (158)	12 (163)	7 (325)

*Too few cases for reliable percentaging.

28). Both these groups are also somewhat more strongly attached to the college they attended and more likely to think it appropriate that their children attend their college. It would also appear that social scientists are slightly more favorably disposed toward their alma mater, even though (as we shall see later) social scientists

TABLE 28   *Attitudes toward college attended, by 1968 career field*

| 1968 career field | Percent in highest quartile | | Percent | |
	Criticism index	Perceived-quality index	Strong emotional attachment to college	Desirable to send children to alma mater
Physical sciences	28	28	31	10
Biological sciences	35	20	16	5
Social sciences	31	25	31	24
Humanities	31	23	28	17
Engineering	27	21	21	18
Medicine	26	55	33	24
Other health	26	26	28	23
Education	31	21	26	17
Business	28	24	27	22
Law	36	41	48	30
Other professions	27	21	26	17

are among those who are most likely to be supporters of radicalism and militancy on the part of students.

College quality, then, seems to be a moderate predictor of favorable attitudes toward one's higher educational experience, with only the Catholic educational institutions standing as an exception. And here the emotional attachment persists, in spite of high levels of criticism of the institutions. The popularity of their higher educational institutions among doctors, lawyers, and social scientists, and among those who attended private universities and liberal arts colleges, seems to be a function of the quality of the college. One therefore is forced to ask whether the events that actually happened in the alumni's lives at the school (or more accurately, the alumni's memories of such events) might be more accurate predictors of their favorable disposition toward the colleges. Table 29 confirms this suspicion. Substantial gamma coefficients exist between favorable attitudes toward the college and the alumni's perceptions of both what their colleges accomplished for them and the attitudes of the faculty and the administration.

The strongest predictor of emotional attachment to the college that one attended is whether the college is perceived as training one to make one's own decisions, the gamma here of .41 being one of the largest to be observed anywhere in this report. Only slightly less important in predicting loyalty to the college are its help in forming friendships, its facilitation of the ability to think and express oneself, its contribution to the development of values and goals, its help in learning how to get along with others, and its expansion of tolerance for people and ideas. On all these items the gamma coefficient is .3 or higher. The least important predictor is the college's training of the respondent for his present job. There are some variations in the order of importance of predictors of the desire to send one's children to one's own college, with value formation showing the strongest relationship (.32) and the ability to think for oneself and to make one's own decisions following just behind. Once again job training is at the bottom of the list. In other words, favorable disposition toward one's alma mater seems to be to a very considerable extent the result of the college's contribution to the intellectual and value development of the alumnus—at least as this contribution is perceived seven years after graduation.

The same high level of correlation is also to be found in the relationship between the goals of faculty and administration as perceived by the alumni and the alumni's favorable disposition toward the college. Somewhat surprisingly, the goal of producing a responsible citizen correlates most strongly with emotional attachment (.34), but assisting students to develop objectivity; serving as a center for the dissemination of new ideas; producing a student whose physical, social, moral, intellectual, and aesthetic potentialities have been cultivated; and training in methods of scholarship, all associate strongly (.28 or higher) with emotional attachment to one's college. Preparing students for a useful career is at the bottom of the list, just as job training was in the top half of the table. Citizenship training is also the strongest predictor (.29) of desire to send one's children to one's own college, and career training is the weakest predictor (.03). Second in importance to citizenship is the perception of the faculty and administration as training the students in objectivity, and third is the faculty and administration's perceived concern about the development of the inner character of the students. The alumni, in other words, are most likely to want to send their children to colleges that they feel were strongly committed to training them in values, citizenship, objectivity, and "well-roundedness."

To summarize the findings in Table 29, decision making, objectivity, value formation, good citizenship, broad general training,

TABLE 29 *Coefficients of association between attitudes toward college attended and perception of college experiences (Gamma)*

Statement	Emotional attachment	Desirable to send children to alma mater
How college affected me:		
Helped me to learn how to make my own decisions	.41	.29
Helped me to form valuable and lasting friendships	.39	.26
Developed my abilities to think and to express myself	.37	.30
Helped me to formulate the values and goals of my life	.36	.32
Helped me to learn how to get along with others	.33	.24
Expanded my tolerance for people and ideas	.30	.23
Helped prepare me for marriage and family life	.29	.25
Prepared me to get ahead in the world	.28	.23
Gave me a broad knowledge of the arts and sciences	.27	.20
Helped me learn practical and effective ways of helping people	.26	.22
Trained me for my present job	.18	.11
Perceived goals of faculty and administration:		
Produce a student who is able to perform his citizenship responsibilities effectively	.34	.29
Assist students to develop objectivity about themselves and their beliefs and hence examine those beliefs critically	.32	.26
Serve as a center for the dissemination of new ideas that will change the society whether those ideas are in science, literature, the arts, or politics	.30	.22

and scholarly competence seem to be those college experiences that are most likely to lead to a favorable recollection of what happened to one during the college years. Successful career training, however, does not seem to win for the institutions of higher education much approbation from their alumni. It may very well be that while career training is not unimportant, it is something that is assumed — almost taken for granted — while other sorts of college experiences, perhaps not so easily taken for granted, are ones that form the basis for the alumnus's reaction to his alma mater.

A comparison of the rank ordering of items in Table 29 and the ranking in Tables 22 and 23 indicates that those items which are the strongest predictors of loyalty to the college or inclination

TABLE 29—
continued

Statement	Emotional attachment	Desirable to send children to alma mater
Produce a well-rounded student, that is, one whose physical, social, moral, intellectual and aesthetic potentialities have all been cultivated	.29	.24
Train students in methods of scholarship, and/or scientific research, and/or creative endeavor	.28	.22
Produce a student who, whatever else may be done to him, has had his intellect cultivated to the maximum	.27	.22
Develop the inner character of students so that they can make sound, correct moral choices	.26	.25
Make a good consumer of the student—a person who is elevated culturally, has good taste, and can make good consumer choices	.22	.19
Make sure the student is permanently affected (in mind and spirit) by the great ideas of the great minds of history	.18	.18
Provide the student with skills, attitudes, contacts, and experiences which maximize the likelihood of his occupying a high status in life and a position of leadership in society	.17	.23
Prepare students specifically for useful careers	.07	.03

to send one's children to one's own college are *not* those which are most likely to be reported as having been actually experienced by the alumni. It would appear, therefore, that there is a bad "fit" between those college experiences which are likely to incline alumni to be favorably disposed toward their colleges and those experiences which they remember as actually happening. Table 30 summarizes this bad fit in the form of rank-order correlations. A ranking of items on their power to predict emotional attachment to college and a ranking on frequency with which alumni report that they were actually affected by their college education produce a positive correlation of .11—a small rank-order correlation by anyone's standards. The other three rank-order correlations in Table 30 are negative. There is a very substantial —.43 rank-order correlation between those perceived goals of faculty and administration that are most likely to predict emotional attachment to college and the frequency with which the alumni reported they actually

TABLE 30
Rank-order correlations between strength of experience as a predictor of attitudes toward college and frequency with which experience is reported (Spearman's rho)

Attitude	College affected me	Perceived goals of faculty and administration
Emotional attachment to college	.11	−.43
Desirable to send children to alma mater	−.13	−.20

perceived such goals as being pursued by faculty and administration. In other words, the alumni are least likely to perceive as having happened those experiences that are most likely to dispose them favorably toward their college, and most likely to perceive as having happened those events that are least likely to dispose them favorably toward their college.

The poorness of fit (described in Table 30) ought to be disturbing to American educators. Their accomplishments that are rated most highly are those which alumni view as unimportant; the accomplishments that are rated least highly are those which alumni would really like to see achieved. Any organization that satisfies its clients on minor matters and does not satisfy them on major matters has serious problems.

Another way of getting at this poorness of fit is to ask whether a similarity between the goals one expects of higher education and the goals one actually felt were achieved in one's higher educational experience correlate with favorable attitudes toward the college. Two indices were constructed to measure this variable. The first, called *goal attainment,* was made by scoring each respondent on the number of goals of higher education he considered to be important which he said were actually achieved in his educational experience. The second dimension, called *goal congruence,* was made by scoring each respondent on the number of educational values that he thought should have been of absolute importance to his faculty and administration which were, he thought, of absolute importance to them. A high score on these indices would indicate a great deal of satisfaction with one's higher educational experience, and a low score would indicate a great amount of dissatisfaction.

TABLE 31
Coefficients of association between goal-attainment and goal-congruence indices and background variables (Gamma)

Background variable	Goal-attainment index	Goal-congruence index
College quality	—.07	.10
College size	—.13	—.12
Control (private)	.05	.21
College grades	.01	—.05
Sex (male)	—.27	—.17
Age	—.08	—.08

Table 31 shows that women and those who went to small colleges score higher on goal-attainment satisfaction than do men and those who went to large colleges. On the index of goal congruence, higher scores are achieved by those who went to high-quality colleges, those who went to small colleges, those who went to private colleges, and women. The graduates of high-quality, small, private institutions, particularly if they were women, apparently found a great deal of congruence between what they thought were appropriate values for higher education and the values they perceived to be motivating their faculty and administrators.

As one might expect, high scores on these two indices correlate very strongly with both emotional attachment to college and the desire to send one's children to one's own college. In all instances correlations are in excess of .3 (Table 32). There is a small negative association between high scores on these indices and a favorable attitude toward student militancy.

In other words, it is not merely the fact that one attends a high-quality college that guarantees loyalty to it. It is also the fact that one has perceived the college as being of high quality and has fur-

TABLE 32
Coefficients of association between goal-attainment and goal-congruence indices and higher educational attitudes (Gamma)

Attitude	Goal-attainment index	Goal-congruence index
Emotional attachment to college	.37	.37
Desirable to send children to alma mater	.31	.32
Favorable to student militancy	—.05	—.03

TABLE 33
Coefficients of association between emotional attachment to college and indices of college goals (Gamma)

Indices	Emotional attachment
Career-training index	—.02
Intellectual index	.08

ther perceived that the values and goals of the institution are the same as one's own values and goals.

The relationship between subjective values and objective experiences is confirmed by what we note in Table 33. There is very little connection between scores on the career-training and intellectual indices of values about college goals and attachment to one's college. But Table 34 does show that the combination of values and experience is important. Thus, as one might expect, training for a job predicts a favorable disposition toward the college for those who think that a college should provide career training, but not especially for those who score low on such an index. Similarly, cultivation of the intellect is strongly related to a favorable disposition toward the higher educational institution for those who score high on the intellectual index, but is weakly related to a favorable disposition among those who score low.

As can be seen in Table 35, for those who score high on the intellectual index, the spread of the proportion strongly attached to the college runs from 53 percent for those who thought their faculty and administration considered intellectual training of abso-

TABLE 34
Coefficients of association between attitudes toward college attended and perception of college experiences, by indices of college goals (Gamma)

Indices	Emotional attachment and	Desirable to send children to alma mater and
Career-training index:	*Trained me for my present job*	
High	.28	.18
Low	.12	.03
Intellectual index:	*Intellect cultivated to the maximum*	
High	.42	.36
Low	.12	.10

TABLE 35 *Attitudes toward college attended, by intellectual index and perception of college experience (Percent)*

Intellectual index	Cultivation of intellect was of				
	Absolute top importance	Great importance	Medium importance	Little importance	No importance
	Strong attachment to college				
High	53	39	23	14	12
	(278)	(1,202)	(1,234)	(386)	(74)
Low	22	34	22	22	20
	(95)	(617)	(1,748)	(895)	(191)
	Desirable to send children to alma mater				
High	34	26	16	7	3
	(277)	(1,214)	(1,214)	(388)	(74)
Low	28	24	16	18	12
	(95)	(608)	(1,749)	(903)	(190)

lute top importance to 12 percent for those who thought their faculty and administration considered the development of the intellect of no importance. However, among those who score low on the intellectual index, the spread is merely from 22 percent to 20 percent. Similarly, in the matter of sending one's children to one's alma mater, the spread of those who are high on the intellectual index runs from 34 percent to 3 percent and for those who are low, merely from 28 percent to 12 percent. In other words, it is not just what one has experienced in college that shapes one's disposition toward one's alma mater but one's experience combined with one's particular values and goals about higher education.

In Table 36 we turn to the very complicated question of the relative impact of career field, type of college attended, and college experience on one's favorable disposition toward one's alma mater. Since Table 36 is very complex, an explanation should be given on how to read it. The numbers in the table represent not percentages but *relationships*—that is, the degree of association between two variables. The variables for the associations being considered are attitudes toward the college as manifested by the desirability of one's children attending one's own college and one's emotional attachment to the college, on the one hand, and the effectiveness of the college in having achieved certain goals—career training, intellectual cultivation, and formation of values—on the other. These associations then are given for each of five college types

TABLE 36
Coefficients of association between attitudes toward college attended and perception of college experiences, by 1968 career field and type of college attended (Gamma)

| Type of college attended | Desirable to send children to alma mater | | | |
| | 1968 career field | | | |
	Arts and sciences	Professions	Education	Business
	Trained me for my present job			
University	.16	—.03	.14	.05
Protestant	.28	.24	.22	.11
State	.42	.79	.21	.13
Catholic	.49	.09	.22	.24
Liberal arts	—.43	—.54	—. 34	—.23
	Helped me to formulate values			
University	.29	.23	.25	.28
Protestant	.45	.38	.19	.38
State	.28	.44	.08	.31
Catholic	.53	.42	.17	.51
Liberal arts	—.13	—.32	—.05	.23
	Intellect cultivated to the maximum			
University	.20	.27	.14	.23
Protestant	.27	.26	.20	—.06
State	.06	.54	.18	.30
Catholic	.51	.38	.31	.07
Liberal arts	.30	.16	.05	.23

(university, Protestant, state, Catholic, and liberal arts) and four career orientations (arts and sciences, professions, education, and business). Thus, the first gamma coefficient in the first column means that, among the arts and sciences careerists who attended universities, there is a positive association between a desire to send one's child to one's alma mater and the fact that one perceived one's college as providing career training. On the other hand, the —.23 coefficient in the fifth row of the fourth column of the table means that there is a negative association between having received career training and desiring to send one's child to one's alma mater among businessmen who went to liberal arts colleges. In other words, each number in the table indicates the relationship between

	Strong attachment to college		
	1968 career field		
Arts and sciences	Professions	Education	Business
	Trained me for my present job		
.20	.13	.13	.00
.63	.27	.47	.32
.30	.46	.30	.04
.37	.13	.39	.17
—.18	—.35	—.23	—.30
	Helped me to formulate values		
.43	.36	.25	.29
.46	.28	.20	.51
.55	.31	.22	.56
.44	.57	.48	.37
.10	.36	—.23	.67
	Intellect cultivated to the maximum		
.20	.33	.33	.15
.45	.24	.20	.35
—.03	.27	.28	.43
.20	.36	.34	.03
.31	.59	.22	.63

college experience and attitude toward the college for members of a given profession from a given type of institution. Career-training experience makes the arts and sciences careerists from universities sympathetic to the idea of sending their children to the same college they attended, while it has the opposite effect on businessmen from liberal arts colleges.

The following assertions may be made based on Table 36:

1 For all those in arts and sciences careers, there is a fairly strong positive association between the college's success in providing career training and a favorable attitude toward the college, save for those arts and sciences careerists who went to liberal arts colleges.

2 Only cultivation of the intellect seems consistently to predict favorable disposition toward higher educational institutions for those who attended liberal arts colleges.

3 While all three experiences—career training, intellectual cultivation, and value formation—predict favorable dispositions for professional men, value formation and intellectual cultivation seem much stronger predictors than career training, no matter what kind of institution one attended.

4 For businessmen, value formation seems to be the strongest predictor of sympathetic attitudes toward one's alma mater, quite independently of what kind of higher educational institution one attended.

5 For those whose careers are in education, career training and intellectual development seem, generally speaking, to be stronger predictors of favorable attitudes toward one's college experience than does value formation, though the differences here are less clear-cut.

6 In summary, then, save for those who attended a liberal arts college, career choice seems to have greater impact on which experiences make one favorably disposed toward one's higher educational institution than does the kind of institution one attended. This summary ought not to be particularly surprising, in view of the fact that Table 35 demonstrated that values about higher education reinforced the predictive powers of experiences in college and that Chapter 2 reported that one's values about higher education are closely connected with one's career.

VALUE FORMATION

One final problem remains. It was noted earlier that despite the highly critical attitudes the graduates of Catholic colleges had toward their schools, they nonetheless seemed to be very strongly attached to their institutions and also most likely of all alumni to plan to send their children to the college they had attended. Given the fact that Catholic colleges stress value formation and the additional fact that the formation of values is the strongest predictor of sending one's children to one's own college and a very powerful predictor of emotional attachment, one might wonder whether the rather surprising reaction of the graduates of Catholic colleges to their higher educational experience may be related to their value-oriented goals. Tables 37 and 38 confirm, at least in part, this suspicion. Among those who reported that their college helped them greatly in the formation of values, graduates of private universities, Catholic colleges, and liberal arts colleges were most likely to be strongly attached (Table 37). While the value formation that occurs in these three different kinds of institutions may be quite different (the Catholic colleges focusing more on religious values and the

Type of college attended	Helped to form values	
	Greatly	Not greatly
University (large public)	46	26
	(270)	(1,337)
University (private)	64	26
	(151)	(705)
University (other)	29	19
	(58)	(469)
Protestant (low quality)	42	19
	(192)	(443)
Protestant (high quality)	30	22
	(169)	(789)
State college	32	13
	(203)	(1,175)
Catholic	51	26
	(323)	(541)
Liberal arts college	54	32
	(90)	(210)

high-quality private colleges and universities focusing on humanistic values), it does seem safe to assume that the relative equality in popularity among these three institutions is related to their value-forming functions. Among those respondents who report that their values were not greatly affected by their college experience, only those who attended liberal arts colleges report an unusually high level of emotional attachment.

In Table 38 the findings of Table 37 are replicated with two modifications—in addition to the private universities, the liberal arts colleges, and the Catholic colleges, the Protestant colleges also seem to have fostered attitudes that would incline alumni to send their children to their own alma mater. Secondly, it is precisely those Catholics who report great influence on value formation who are the most likely of any of the alumni to say that it would be desirable to send their children to the college they attended, while Catholics who report relatively little influence on value formation are not notably different from other respondents in plans for their children's higher education.

Despite fairly high levels of criticism by their alumni, Catholic colleges are very likely to attract strong alumni loyalty, perhaps because they have been successful in promoting value formation.

Type of college attended	Helped to form values	
	Greatly	*Not greatly*
University (large public)	20 (271)	17 (1,342)
University (private)	33 (151)	20 (685)
University (other)	18 (66)	12 (467)
Protestant (low quality)	32 (198)	14 (428)
Protestant (high quality)	31 (172)	14 (793)
State college	16 (212)	11 (1,184)
Catholic	41 (325)	21 (529)
Liberal arts college	31 (91)	26 (196)

Furthermore, the "low-quality" Protestant colleges (presumably the ones with the strongest religious ties) are most likely to be criticized by their alumni but are also quite popular with those alumni who report that these colleges influenced their value formation.

One can only conclude that, for all their weaknesses and difficulties, the religiously affiliated schools do have one commodity which the alumni value very highly—the help they offer the young person in formulating his values and his goals in life.

THE ALUMNI SPEAK FOR THEMSELVES Many of the alumni offered extremely thoughtful and sensitive responses to an open-ended question about what their college education meant to them.

A housewife in Cambridge, Massachusetts said:

Perhaps I am an exception, but I found my graduate school experience much more beneficial than my undergraduate—in terms of developing a value system, getting to know myself and society, and specific training for my teaching career. A person at the age of 18–20 simply has not lived long enough away from home and more importantly in the "real" world outside of academe to be able to make too many earth-shaking insights. Undergraduate school did help me, though—a large university of 20,000+ students exposes you to ideas and people different from

your particular mold. However, the pressure at my school for social smooth-
ness (Greek life), excellent grades, etc. greatly diminished the possibilities
of my developing a personal and creative awareness of the world of ideas.
Large size, of course, also prevented my education from being as partici-
pative (instead of repetitive) as it might have been. I was sporadically
"turned on," but not enough—which of course is not strictly the university's fault. I myself had not matured sufficiently to be able to place a more
sensible perspective on all the things flowing around me.

And a Jewish businessman from New York City even had a
quote from Dostoevski to back up his attitudes:

Upon reflection, I am very disappointed with my college education. For
four years I worked pretty hard to memorize a lot of facts and concepts
which I have since forgotten. I emerged from college, therefore, essentially
the same bewildered young man who hoped college would teach him the
answers to some of the riddles of life and being. College was useful only
in that it taught me how to think in a somewhat logical fashion. Profes-
sionally, and I use the word very loosely, I took a course in public relations
in college which bears absolutely no relationship to P.R. as it is practiced
by me and my colleagues daily.

College is supposed to teach a person how to think and how to live. A
person must learn the *meaning of life,* and unless a person learns this he
will be unhappy forever, and will probably make others unhappy. My college tried to mold my intellect, which I have since realized is not man's most
important faculty. Man's spirit, his soul, is totally neglected by college just
as it is neglected by our materialistic world, and as a character in "Kara-
mazov" says, "Without God anything is possible." And now we are wit-
nessing the world crumbling around us simply because man has lost sight
of his true essence, his soul.

I am very unhappy about the materialistic, money-grubbing world I live
in, but I am optimistic, because the kids of today seem to have an understanding of their essence and of morality. They and the priests are fighting
to save a world that reviles them and puts them in prison. It seems that
America's best are put in jail these days, and the racist, Capitalist baboons
are calling all the shots. The elections this November will tell the story.

And the universities, which have become indoctrination centers for
materialism and Capitalism, are in large measure responsible for the mess
America is in today. I always dug my professors; the administrative ap-
paratus is at fault.

A teacher at a Catholic university honestly discussed the
strengths and weaknesses of her undergraduate experience:

As a graduate student and college teacher, I have found that my college education prepared me well in most areas. I received a good formal education, knew good teachers from whom I could learn—at least by imitation—had good classroom experiences which I can try to reproduce for my own students. The preparation for scholarly work was, of course, excellent. But there is one area in which I was *not* prepared: I am not prepared to deal with or even to think intelligently about the current "revolutionary" movement on college campuses—e.g., Columbia. Since people of the generation of my teachers have been unable to deal well, this is not surprising. But I am appalled that such disaffection and alienation have grown at the same time that my friends and I have been happily studying and teaching. For the first time I feel the existence of a generation gap between me (age 28) and my undergraduate students. I am trying to devise intellectually honest ways of bridging that gap.

A woman from Pennsylvania reported that her college training had a deep impact on her social awareness:

My college education laid the foundation for most of my serious thinking about society, my part in it, and helped me learn a great deal about myself. I do wish I had taken a course or two in creative self-expression and also wish that the role of housewife-mother-contributor to community in a non-professional way was included in some series of courses. I truly believe that too many college educated women are busy in their professions while their children are experiencing a strange kind of neglect.

And a housewife from New Jersey lamented the absence of meaningful goals in her higher educational experience:

I feel very strongly the lack of a meaningful goal which will be personally satisfying. How much of this I can blame on my college education and how much is the result of my own personality and disposition I cannot say— I have great difficulty in dealing with people which I thought I would grow out of in college but didn't. This is quite probably a major cause of my job dissatisfaction. I feel that it would have been very helpful if when I was in college the following two opportunities were available—1, a work and school program, i.e., six months work or on the job training with pay followed by six months on campus again, and 2, some sort of counselor with realism, concern and understanding, perhaps even a therapist. Perhaps a combination of the two items above would have oriented and trained me better. Item 1 would have certainly eased my financial discomfort. Sometimes it seems to me we were asked to choose a major; we fulfilled the program requirements and stepped out in the real world to discover ourselves totally ignorant about how things really are.

At the same time I do not feel a college should specifically be a trade school, and I agree that college training should be general. But I would like to say one thing as a generalist, it makes it damn difficult to get a job.

In grammar school they asked me what did I want to do. I didn't know. The same in high school, in college, after college, and after an M.S. The only thing I know is to go back for a PhD. and I fear the result would be the same then. I may be lost—but I'm not alone—there are others in the same boat.

And a gentleman from Colorado used his own experience as a teacher to evaluate the performance of his teachers:

After four years of teaching I realize most teachers know little of life and transfer their hang-ups to their students as much as they can. Remedy: human beings as teachers.

My own teachers rarely broke through to my soul—and it can be done, even *in* a class. But I doubt if college can prepare people for teaching or if most teachers can help people to feel honestly.

Some respondents were less critical of their colleges. A housewife in Wyoming said:

It developed me as a person, increasing my sense of security and my value to society. It helped me to get insight into my behavior and I have related to others, thus improving my ability to meet people. It established rapport and work with them in giving and receiving situations.

A librarian at a military academy said favorable things about his curriculum: "Of great value was Basic College, a program of studies in social science, humanities, communication skills and natural science required for completion by all students by the end of their sophomore year."

And a surgeon said: "College was excellent. It certainly broadened my views, had outstanding faculty. Fairly large and impersonal but this could be tolerated. . . . Prepared me well for medicine through its pre-med course."

A high school English teacher said: "Perhaps most important of all, I learned self-discipline and how to read for enjoyment. I believe the complete change from the very urban (home) to the very rural (campus) also widened my views of our country."

And a female member of the faculty at a Big Ten university said: "My undergraduate days were vitally important in forming the person I am now. The enrichment I gained from forming life-long friendships with the faculty in my area of theatre could never be replaced."

Other respondents, though, had more mixed reactions. A professor from the East Coast said of her school:

I did feel alienated there until I could participate in campus political affairs. There was not as much contact with professors as I would have liked, but the political life with my fellow students *prepared me* very well to be a college professor.

One suspects that this is what the sociologist would call a latent function of higher education—but a latent one that is not without importance.

A New York housewife found college helped her to overcome her lack of self-confidence, but not completely:

Prior to college I had little opportunity to present my views and/or opinions to others, but I did so in college. Formal and informal discussions showed I was able to communicate my ideas to others. . . . However I dated little or not at all, thereby missing the casual relationship with males. . . . I find I must know people, especially men, for awhile before I am at ease with them.

A housewife from Ohio saw both good and bad elements in the liberal education she received:

College not sufficiently concerned with conditions outside its walls—too narrow in outlook. But preparation for graduate work was excellent, as was the general intellectual atmosphere. The liberal arts background I received is far more important now than specific career training might have been. My education was very well rounded and I feel, as a result, that I too am well rounded, comfortable in any situation.

Another housewife—this one from Wisconsin—made the following comments about her college:

1. Provided time and place for serious considerations of big issues of human life.
2. Exposed me to other possibilities for manner of life I might choose.
3. Not frequent enough demand on my own expression of what I was learning.

A high school teacher from South Dakota, while admitting that college helped him to live a "full life," added: "At times I feel I fell short and did not take advantage of all that was offered. Possibly a lack of all the arts and influence of culture events has some effect on my present need."

Some respondents were quite critical of their alma mater's failure to challenge them intellectually. An Indiana English teacher observed:

I regret that my university provided so little intellectual excitement. Faculty members went about their academic interests and professional business in craftsmanlike ways, but seldom brought any possibility for the life of the mind to their classrooms or the campus at large.

And another professor, this one from Massachusetts, said: "College was only superficial. I never had to learn deeply, i.e., understand. It has left holes in my background that my professional activities now virtually preclude filling." A research associate of a science center observed: "I do feel more stress could have been put on developing curiosity and desire to know more just for the satisfaction of knowing instead of making a good grade."

However, the most serious criticisms leveled at the schools had to do with their failure to promote communications and their unreality to the world outside. A systems analyst from Ohio said:

The greatest shortcoming is the difficulty of communication—both written and verbal. I think I concentrated on courses which taught "techniques." I should have spent more time studying people and human behavior than history, English literature, sociology, etc.

And a counseling psychologist in California said that his college was "irrelevant to life and personal concerns, too performance oriented, too much ivory tower." A housewife from Oregon observed: "The only fault I can find is that [my college] community is an idealistic one and I found adjusting to the world outside difficult at times and often disappointing." A chemistry teacher in an oriental university said that her college was "seriously lacking in *reality* of personal and academic experiences." A teacher in a Lutheran parochial high school commented that her school failed " . . . in preparing the students for living and competing in the outside world. Being a church college in a small town, it sheltered us from the outside world."

A specialist in programming and information in Michigan concluded:

> Not only the class of '61, but I am sure the class of '68 will not have been properly prepared for the challenges to be faced. The greatest needs today are for communication and understanding. No university, to my knowledge, prepares its students to deal with the complexities of the revolutionary society in which we live. Less emphasis on grades and more on people and ideas and our students would be better prepared.

And finally, an Episcopal priest said, somewhat enigmatically: "It is perhaps unfortunate that college should be wasted on the age group dominated by passion."

When permitted to speak in their own words, then, college alumni seem most likely both to criticize and to praise the schools for their contribution to the development of their total personality. They are part of the personalist generation and they evaluate college in personalist terms. Both career preparation and intellectual formation, as well as the "well-roundedness" of the personality, are expected to contribute to a higher goal—the effective performance of the person in a complex society.

As one colleague remarked after reading the previous pages, "A college is supposed to be a family, a church, a home, and a psychiatrist. With such expectations, it's a wonder that all colleges haven't been blown up long ago." However facetious the remark, it still conveys an important point. Alumni expectations seem to exceed the capacity of any human institution. If colleges are only very moderately loved by their alumni, part of the explanation may be that the alumni blame colleges for not being the sorts of institutions that it is quite impossible for them to be. The great faith of Americans in the power of higher education may have made them very naïve about what education can accomplish. To the extent that the colleges and universities have not attempted to reduce the level of naïveté, they have contributed to a situation in which the clientele of higher education will almost certainly be disappointed by what has taken place during the higher educational experience.

On the other hand, if educators can legitimately plead for more realism from their clientele in defining what college ought to be, they must acknowledge that the clientele is merely reflecting the goals of higher education that the educators have set for themselves.

Thus, while higher education continues to try to improve its service to its clientele, it probably must resign itself to the fact that idealized expectations on both the side of educators and the side of the educated may turn the higher educational institution into something of an inkblot.

One of the more striking findings in this chapter should be emphasized again: One's memory of one's college experience is quite subjective. That is, our alumni are not favorably disposed toward institutions mainly because the institutions are objectively of high quality; nor does the size, ownership, or control of the college have much relevance in the alumni's present reaction to the colleges they attended. The important predictors of a favorable disposition toward one's alma mater concern how the college was subjectively perceived, and particularly whether it was perceived as contributing to the educational goals and values that the alumnus now thinks are important to higher education. If someone should approach one of our alumni and insist that he went to a fine institution because that institution scores high on Astin's index, the alumnus would agree with such an evaluation, provided he felt that his own experiences at the college had corresponded to his presently stated values about the purposes of higher education. But if he did not feel that the college had contributed to the goals that he presently thinks valuable, then he would not be very impressed by its rating on the Astin index. The Catholic colleges that presumably did not score in the upper levels on Astin's index still have relatively loyal alumni precisely because these colleges were able to accomplish what their graduates—and what most other alumni, too—seem to think is of critical importance in their higher educational experience. The apparently low level of affection for the college that one attended seems to be decisively related to the college's failure to achieve the goals that the alumnus considers important.

SUMMARY AND CONCLUSION

Four principal findings, all of them related, emerge from this chapter:

1. Intellectual and cultural experiences are extremely important in determining the attitudes of alumni toward the colleges they attended.

2. Alumni think that colleges are better at those things which the alumni think least important and not so good at those things which they think most important.

3. Generally speaking, the kind of career choice one has made is more closely

related to the values that dispose one favorably toward one's higher educational institution than is the type of college attended.

4   Despite item 3, however, Catholic colleges, Protestant colleges, liberal arts colleges, and private universities do seem to earn considerable popularity among those alumni who feel that value formation was an important part of their college education. In the case of the Catholics, this is true despite a high level of criticism of the quality and the student life of the college.

Educators might well be excused from being ambivalent about these findings. Presumably, they would be inclined to rejoice over the fact that the alumni are willing to take seriously the intellectual and value-oriented goals of higher education—values and goals that probably to some very considerable extent they learned from the institutions themselves. Furthermore, educators should be delighted that it is precisely the intellectual and value experiences that are most likely to predict favorable dispositions toward the institution a respondent attended. On the other hand, one presumes that educators will be somewhat uneasy about the finding that there is a very poor fit between those experiences which satisfy their "clients" and those experiences which the clients perceive as actually having occurred. An educator might ruefully remark that the alumni seem to take the goals of educators more seriously than they perceive the educators themselves taking such goals. The practical conclusion one could draw from this phenomenon would be that while the other aims of higher education can surely not be neglected, the intellectual and value-oriented aims seem to be the most important ones to be emphasized, at least in terms of client satisfaction. The lesson of the Catholic colleges that were able to compensate for many weaknesses because of their contribution to value formation might be taken as extremely important for the rest of American higher education.

5. Reform of Higher Education

A fairly large number of questions were posed to alumni from which one might deduce their suggestions for reform. They were asked what courses they would like to have taken, what activities they would like to have engaged in, whether a moratorium in the college experience would be a good idea, what they thought of more student power, and what kinds of colleges they desired for their children. In addition, they were given an opportunity to express in their own words what changes they would like to see take place in higher education.

COURSES ALUMNI WOULD TAKE NOW The respondents were presented with an extensive list of college courses and asked to choose the courses that they would be most likely to take if they were given the opportunity once again. As Table 39 indicates, the humanities were the overwhelming first choice of the respondents, with education coming next. The social sciences and business were tied for third with 14 percent, and 13 percent said that they would be interested in courses in the physical or biological sciences. Of the 100-odd courses presented in the questionnaires, the single most popular was fine arts, which was chosen by more than 10 percent of the respondents. It is interesting to note that while only 17 percent of the alumni have careers in the humanities and social sciences, 45 percent of them would take courses in these disciplines. Clearly the alumni are voting strongly in favor of the humanistic disciplines in the popularity poll of courses they would like to take if they were given a chance now.

Granting that the alumni are extraordinarily attracted to the humanities when asked about the courses they would take if they had the opportunity to do it again, one still wonders whether the quality of the school one attended, one's intellectual accomplish-

69

TABLE 39
First choice of course alumni would have taken that they did not take

First course	Percent
Humanities	31
Education	15
Social sciences	14
Business	14
Physical sciences	9
Biological sciences	4
Engineering	3
Other	10
TOTAL	100

ments, and one's career choice affect this decision. We observe in Table 40 that even those who go to the lowest-quality colleges still endorse humanities as their most popular course, although they are some 20 percentage points less likely to endorse humanities than those who went to the highest-quality schools. Business courses are more popular in the low-quality colleges than in the high-quality colleges, while education has almost no popularity at all among the alumni of the better colleges and considerable popularity among the alumni of the poorer colleges. Popularity of the social sciences seems to be relatively constant across college quality. In other words, those who went to the best colleges and

TABLE 40 *College quality and first choice of courses alumni would take if they had the opportunity now (Percent)*

College quality	Physical sciences	Biological sciences	Social sciences	Humanities	Engineering	Medicine	Other health	Education	Business	Law	Other professions	Total Percent	N
High	11	4	18	46	2	2	0	5	9	1	3	101	312
	9	2	16	37	4	0	0	6	17	2	6	99	583
	9	5	16	36	3	1	1	10	13	1	5	100	1,052
	9	4	14	31	2	1	1	16	12	2	8	100	2,169
	8	7	12	21	4	1	2	18	18	2	7	100	1,094
	8	3	13	32	4	0	2	18	13	0	8	101	1,148
Low	7	3	11	27	3	0	1	22	14	3	8	99	586

TABLE 41 *Sex and first choice of courses alumni would take if they had the opportunity now (Percent)*

					First choice of courses								
Sex	Physical sciences	Biological sciences	Social sciences	Humanities	Engineering	Medicine	Other health	Education	Business	Law	Other professions	Total Percent	N
Male	11	4	13	26	5	1	1	8	22	2	6	99	3,976
Female	5	5	14	38	0	1	1	24	3	0	8	99	2,968

were most likely to be exposed to courses in the humanities are the ones most likely to want more such courses. Those who went to the poorer quality colleges still are more likely to want humanities courses than anything else, even though they probably had relatively few humanities courses in their educational experience. Vocational courses (education, business) are more popular in the schools in which they were more likely to be given than in the schools in which they were less likely to be given, but in general the combination of education and business surpasses the popularity of the humanities only in colleges of rather low quality.

Physical science courses are more popular with men than with women (Table 41), and the humanities are more popular with women than with men. As one might expect, the desire for more courses in engineering seems to be limited to males, while women are more inclined to seek more education courses and men are more

TABLE 42 *College grades and first choice of courses alumni would take if they had the opportunity now (Percent)*

					First choice of courses								
College grades	Physical sciences	Biological sciences	Social sciences	Humanities	Engineering	Medicine	Other health	Education	Business	Law	Other professions	Total Percent	N
A	13	4	18	45	1	2	1	6	5	1	4	100	540
B	10	4	15	34	3	0	1	14	12	1	6	100	3,749
C	6	3	11	25	4	1	2	18	18	2	9	99	2,565
D	0	0	0	20	10	0	0	10	20	20	20	100	10

Type of college attended	First choice of courses					
	Physical sciences	*Biological sciences*	*Social sciences*	*Humanities*	*Engineering*	*Medicine*
University (large public)	10	4	12	33	4	0
University (private)	9	4	16	37	3	1
University (other)	9	7	13	26	5	1
Protestant (low quality)	8	6	13	26	2	0
Protestant (high quality)	9	6	14	35	1	0
State college	7	3	13	30	2	0
Catholic	7	2	16	28	4	1
Liberal arts college	8	1	18	47	2	1

inclined to seek more business courses. Even among men, however, the humanities courses still are the most popular.

There is a direct relationship (Table 42) between college grades and a preference for courses in the humanities, but even those with a C average prefer the humanities to other possible courses, although business and education courses together are more popular than the humanities in the C group.

The popularity of humanities courses is greatest among the graduates of liberal arts colleges and private universities and is inclined to be least among the graduates of the religiously affiliated schools (Table 43). However, only among the graduates of "low-quality" Protestant colleges and state colleges does education come close to equaling the humanities in popularity. The popularity of the social and physical sciences seems to be fairly constant across all college types.

Finally in Table 44 we observe that a number of career positions are likely to lead their occupants to express a preference for a course in their own career field rather than for a course in the humanities. The physical scientists, the social scientists (though these by only a small margin), the engineers, the educationists, and the businessmen all prefer courses in their own discipline to courses in the humanities. On the other hand, the largest margin of preference for the humanities over one's own professional discipline is

Other health	Education	Business	Law	Other professions	Total	
					Percent	N
2	12	16	1	6	100	1,454
0	8	14	1	6	99	739
2	10	16	2	9	100	464
0	24	10	0	10	99	568
1	15	10	2	8	101	870
2	23	12	2	6	100	1,191
1	16	14	2	8	99	772
2	6	8	1	5	99	273

to be found among the doctors and lawyers, with the M.D.'s being the group most likely (56 percent) to express a preference for a course in the humanities (besides the humanists themselves). Indeed, the M.D.'s are also more likely than anyone but the humanists to choose within the liberal disciplines of the social sciences and the humanities, with about three-quarters of the doctors expressing such a preference.

Just as educational values seem to be a function of one's present career needs and past career training, so it could be said that varying preferences for courses are closely related to these two variables. Doctors and lawyers receive comprehensive training in their own disciplines in graduate school. They are aware that there is little specifically vocational about their undergraduate training and that undergraduate training probably cannot equip them with skills that they need in their professional occupation. As presumably successful and well-to-do professionals, they may feel the need to have cultural interests (even though they probably do not have the time for such interests). Knowing that further courses in medicine and law will not be required for their professional advancement, they can afford to express interest in the humanities and social sciences. Businessmen and educators, on the other hand, probably have received some undergraduate training in their own disciplines and occupy career positions where more educational

TABLE 44
*1968 career
field and first
choice of
courses alumni
would take if
they had the
opportunity now
(Percent)*

1968 career field	First choice of courses					
	Physical sciences	*Biological sciences*	*Social sciences*	*Humanities*	*Engineering*	*Medicine*
Physical sciences	42	10	9	26	3	0
Biological sciences	12	36	5	40	0	0
Social sciences	13	5	38	34	0	0
Humanities	5	2	11	73	0	0
Engineering	16	3	7	19	30	0
Medicine	6	5	18	56	0	3
Other health	1	14	19	33	0	1
Education	6	4	14	29	0	0
Business	8	1	9	20	4	0
Law	7	1	17	40	1	1
Other professions	6	3	20	30	2	1

credits—if not more skills—can be a means for advancement. Therefore, their educational concerns lean more heavily in the direction of career training in the narrow sense of the word. One suspects that if business and education required extensive professional training in graduate school and if the accumulation of more academic training were not necessary for advancement, then the educators and the businessmen would react the same way that doctors and lawyers do.

To summarize the material on the kinds of courses the alumni would take if they had a chance to do it again, the humanities are universally popular and in conjunction with the social sciences attract almost half of the alumni choices. The humanities maintain their popularity with both men and women, graduates of good colleges and poor ones, and bright students and less bright ones; although women, graduates of high-quality colleges, and the alumni with the highest grades are most likely to be sympathetically disposed toward the humanities. However, certain careers (law and medicine) are overwhelmingly sympathetic to the liberal disciplines, while others (notably, education and business) lead respondents to be favorably disposed to more courses in their own field, largely

Other health	Education	Business	Law	Other professions	Total Percent	Total N
0	0	6	0	4	100	265
1	1	4	0	0	99	135
0	4	5	0	2	101	170
0	4	1	0	4	100	366
0	0	20	1	3	99	375
0	4	4	0	3	99	154
7	16	6	0	2	99	247
1	37	2	0	6	99	1,848
1	2	46	4	4	99	1,285
0	3	18	8	4	99	188
0	8	10	1	19	100	837

because such courses provide training and opportunities for occupational advancement. We note that the distinction between general and vocational education is blurred here, as it has been in previous chapters. Those who want more vocational education are precisely those who are not likely to have had formal graduate training in their careers; those who want more general education are those for whom more vocational training is not so pertinent and who may even find the skills and qualities that they attribute to their general education useful for the kind of career they are in.

WHAT THEY WOULD HAVE DONE DIFFERENTLY The humanistic orientation is strongly reinforced by answers to a question on what different kinds of activity the alumni would engage in if they were given a second chance. Table 45 shows that more than half of them voted for reading books not related to specific courses and learning about poetry, art, music, history, philosophy, and English; and almost half cast their vote for learning more about psychology and sociology (48 percent). Given the fairly low level of interest in the arts reported earlier and the feeling of the alumni that colleges did not, in fact, contribute much to their cultural and reading development, one can only conclude

	Would like to have done more
TABLE 45 *What alumni would have done differently (Percent)* / *Item*	
Read books not related to specific courses	57
Learn about poetry, art, or music	53
Learn about history, philosophy, or English	52
Learn about psychology or sociology	48
Study	46
Try to get to know the faculty	43
Participate in extracurricular activities (sports, drama, student government, etc.)	38
Learn about science or mathematics	37
Take course(s) in an area directly related to my present job	37
Participate in activities that were of service to others	36
Read books related to specific courses	35
Date	30
Worry about getting good grades	10

that the opinions recorded in Table 45 are something of a rebuke to American higher education.

It is easy to dismiss the alumni's reaction as a form of posing—and some educators have done so in commenting on preliminary versions of this report. If people want to learn about poetry, art, music, history, philosophy, or English, there is nothing to prevent them from doing so. It may very well be that higher education did not motivate them to such activities when they were in college because no power on heaven or earth could have so motivated them. Nevertheless, it still remains interesting that however nonhumanistic in their activities they may have been when they were in college, they were extremely humanistic in their opinions about college now that they are out of it. It is also quite clear from Table 45 that only a handful (one-tenth) of the students would have worried more about grades if they had it to do over again.

STUDENT INVOLVEMENT The alumni are somewhat sympathetic to the demands of contemporary college students for a greater share of control of the university, but only on certain matters. In Table 46 we observe that two-thirds of the alumni do not think that the college should stay

		Favorable to anti-student position
TABLE 46 *Alumni attitudes toward student involvement (Percent)*	*Statement*	

Statement		Favorable to anti-student position
The students are capable of regulating their own lives and the college should stay out of this area	(Disagree)	66
The college should take the responsibility to see that students do not break the law	(Agree)	55
Students should have the right to protest against recruiters on campus if the students think the recruiters are helping to carry out immoral practices	(Disagree)	47
The college should assume responsibility for a student's behavior just as parents do	(Agree)	45
Rules governing student behavior should be made by the students	(Disagree)	43
Students should make the rules governing their participation in off-campus political activity	(Disagree)	34
Rules governing student behavior should be enforced by students	(Disagree)	27
The college should not try to stop students from taking part in political activity	(Disagree)	17
Students should have the right to participate in decisions on		
Faculty tenure	(Disagree)	82
Admission standards	(Disagree)	80
Tuition and fees	(Disagree)	81
What is taught in specific courses	(Disagree)	58
Organization of the curriculum	(Disagree)	40

completely out of the regulation of student life and that four-fifths are not willing to concede to the students any power on questions of faculty tenure, admission standards, and tuition. Fifty-eight percent are not even ready to yield to students participation in decisions on what is taught in specific courses. (It should be noted that the figures in Table 46 indicate the proportion reacting *against* demands for student involvement.) A bit more than half of the alumni, on the other hand, think that students should have the right to protest against campus recruiters, that colleges should not assume responsibility for a student's behavior just as parents do, and that rules governing student behavior should be made by the students. However, even on these items almost half of the alumni are willing to reject student demands. Substantial support for student involvement can be found only in such matters as the organization of the curriculum, the enforcement of student rules, and the participation of students in off-campus political activity.

We combined the responses to the student-involvement items presented in Table 46 into four indices: *student-politics index, student-control-over-rules index, student-power index,* and *student-freedom index.* The indices contain the following items:

Student-politics index

- The college should not try to stop students from taking part in political activity.
- Students should have the right to protest against recruiters on campus if the students think the recruiters are helping to carry out immoral practices.
- Students should make the rules governing their participation in off-campus political activity.

Student-control-over-rules index

- Rules governing student behavior should be made by the students.
- Rules governing student behavior should be enforced by the students.

Student-power index

Students should have the right to participate in decisions on:

- Faculty tenure
- Organization of the curriculum
- What is taught in specific courses
- Tuition and fees

Student-freedom index

- The college should assume responsibility for a student's behavior just as parents do. (Disagree)
- The students are capable of regulating their own lives and the college should stay out of this area. (Agree)
- The college should take the responsibility to see that students do not break the law. (Disagree)

The quality of college one has attended, one's undergraduate grades, and one's age all have moderate relationships with a high

Background variable	Student-politics index	Rules index	Student-power index	Student-freedom index
College quality	.16	.07	.00	.16
College size	.03	−.06	.00	.09
College grades	.12	.07	.03	.10
Sex (male)	−.03	−.33	−.07	.02
Age	−.14	−.13	−.11	−.08

TABLE 47
Coefficients of association between student-involvement indices and background variables (Gamma)

score on the student-politics index, which measures inclination to give students control over their own political activities. Young students and women are the most inclined to support student control over the formulation and enforcement of the rules, as measured by the rules index (Table 47). On the whole, the relationships between the background variables and the student-power and student-freedom indices are lower. The only correlate with the student-power index above .1 is age (−.11), indicating that the younger alumni are more likely than the older ones to advocate student participation in decision making at colleges. There is no correlation with college quality or size. For the student-freedom index, the highest correlations are .16 with college quality and .10 with grades. Besides those from high-quality colleges and those with good grades, alumni from large colleges and again the younger alumni are more inclined to oppose college regulation of students' lives, as measured by the student-freedom index.

Thus, on the four student-involvement indices, most of the correlations with background variables are low or moderate. Age, grades, and quality of college are the principal correlates with "radical" positions.

Table 48 shows that the graduates of liberal arts colleges, of private universities, and of "high-quality" Protestant colleges are more likely to be favorably disposed to student regulation of political activities. The last group is also the most likely to score high on the index measuring desire for greater student control over rules.

Variations in the highest quartile level for the student-power index are very small. On the student-freedom index, alumni of the universities tend to show greater opposition to regulation, as do alumni of the Protestant colleges of high quality and the liberal arts colleges, while alumni of the Catholic colleges and the state

Type of college attended	Student-politics index	Rules index	Student-power index	Student-freedom index
University (large public)	28	17	23	36
University (private)	37	21	19	36
University (other)	27	13	21	35
Protestant (low quality)	21	13	11	17
Protestant (high quality)	35	25	20	33
State college	18	15	20	21
Catholic	28	14	22	23
Liberal arts college	33	21	18	32

colleges seem to feel less opposed, and those from "low-quality" Protestant colleges are least opposed to the college regulating the lives of students.

As we might expect by now (Table 49), the alumni in the humanities and the social sciences are the ones most in sympathy with the thrust for student involvement, and alumni in business and engineering are the least likely to support it. Somewhat striking, however, is the fact that on the student-politics index and the student-freedom index, those with legal career choices tend to be quite sympathetic to the goals of more student control, perhaps because

1968 career field	Student-politics index	Rules index	Student-power index	Student-freedom index
Physical sciences	31	15	24	40
Biological sciences	40	13	28	33
Social sciences	53	17	35	51
Humanities	52	32	28	42
Engineering	20	12	16	33
Medicine	39	19	19	28
Other health	14	24	30	24
Education	26	20	22	21
Business	20	11	13	25
Law	36	15	18	42
Other professions	34	16	25	35

	Opinion	Percent

TABLE 50
Alumni opinions on higher education

Opinion	Percent
Students should go through college:	
As fast as possible	39
Take time off:	
Between high school and college	32
After college entrance	29
College education is a benefit to a woman in her capacity as housewife and mother:	
Great benefit	58
Great or some benefit	96

their own sense of due process and representation makes it difficult for them to accept some of the current campus disciplinary practices.[1]

While the alumni population is about evenly divided on student protest,[2] they are only willing to support the specific demands of the current student protesters in a limited number of areas generally concerning enforcement of rules, off-campus political behavior, and the organization of the curriculum. Most sympathetic to the goals of student protesters were the younger alumni, the graduates of high-quality colleges, those who had spent several years in graduate school, and those with career choices in the humanities, with the social sciences and, rather surprisingly, law coming next.

MISCELLANEOUS OPINIONS From Table 50 we learn that a surprisingly large number of alumni (more than three-fifths) do not think it necessary for students to go immediately through college. Roughly half of those supporting a moratorium think it should come between high school and college, and the other half think it should come during college. Given the fact that American higher education only very reluctantly provides such a moratorium and that the larger society penalizes males who seek such a moratorium by drafting them, one can see that the alumni are recommending a fairly substantial educational and social reform.

[1] It should be remembered at this point that what we are measuring are not the attitudes that our alumni had in college, but rather their attitudes at the present time toward the demands for student power that are being made by the current generation of undergraduates.

[2] A more detailed consideration of this will be given in Chapter 6.

TABLE 51
Alumni opinion
on taking time
off during
educational
sequence by
having taken
time off
(Percent)

Took time off	Time off would be beneficial		
	Yes	*No*	*Total*
During college:			
Yes	73	27	100
No	58	42	100
Between high school and college:			
Yes	81	19	100
No	58	42	100

Those who themselves had a moratorium between high school and college or during college are, as one might expect, more favorably disposed to providing such opportunities than those who did not take time off. However, even a majority of the latter group think that such an opportunity would be beneficial (Table 51). If one assumes that this sort of value will be inculcated in the children of the alumni, it seems fairly clear that as the present century draws to a close, there will have to be a drastic change in the systems of bookkeeping and accounting in the American higher educational enterprise. The young person who graduates at 21 after four years of college may become less and less typical.

Returning to Table 50, we see that approximately three-fifths of the alumni are also willing to endorse the proposition that an education for a woman is of great benefit to her in her role as a wife and mother, and only a handful are ready to assert that it is of no benefit at all. It is a long jump from such an opinion to saying that the 1961 alumni are ardent feminists (and our colleague, Alice Rossi, in her work has demonstrated that they are not), but the alumni at least are capable of seeing a relationship between higher education and the successful fulfillment of the wife-and-mother role.

COLLEGE FOR THEIR CHILDREN

Another way of determining what the alumni think higher education should be like is to ask the respondents what kind of education they would like to provide for their oldest child of their same sex. Tables 52, 53, and 54 provide information on this topic. Cost seems to be of relatively little importance, while academic standing and training for graduate school appear of great importance (Table 52). Even though only three-fourths of them think that a good general

	Absolute top importance	Absolute top or great importance
TABLE 52 Importance of choosing college with certain characteristics for oldest child of same sex as respondent (Percent) — *Characteristics*		
The costs of attending the college are low	1	12
The college has a very high academic standing	24	82
The college provides excellent training for graduate or professional school	14	61

education is "very desirable" and only about half would say that career training is "very desirable," it still must be noted that 87 percent think that career training is at least a "somewhat desirable" characteristic to be found in the college for their children (Table 53). In other words, the alumni show some indication of wanting to have

TABLE 53 Desirability of college with certain characteristics for oldest child of same sex as respondent (Percent) — *Characteristics*	Very desirable	Very or somewhat desirable
The college offers a good general education	77	98
The college gives good career training	48	87
The faculty and administration are concerned with students' personality development	36	84
The college gives students a lot of personal freedom	12	53
The college gives a good religious education	10	34
Students can join fraternities or sororities	8	35
The college is close to home	7	40
There is an extensive athletic program at the college	6	36
The college has students who are of the same social background as my child	5	35
It is the same college I graduated from	2	19

TABLE 54
Desired college size for oldest son and oldest daughter (Percent)

College size	Oldest son	Oldest daughter
Under 2,000	26	35
2,000–4,999	34	32
5,000–9,999	23	19
10,000 or more	16	13

their cake and eat it too. They want a good general education more strongly than they want career training, but they still want career training. However, as we noted previously, it would seem that for many of the alumni there is no opposition between these two characteristics of the higher educational institution because many of them saw general education as a form of career training for themselves.

The only other characteristic of the college that was considered "very desirable" by a substantial number of the alumni is that the college be concerned with the personality development of its students. When one adds the proportion who think that this goal is "somewhat desirable," then one has some indication of the alumni's reply to those educators who argue that it is only the intellectual development of the student that is a proper concern of the college or the university. Approximately one-half of the respondents think it would be at least desirable that the college "give students a lot of personal freedom."

Finally, to repeat a statistic from the previous chapter, only 2 percent of the alumni think that it is "very desirable" that their children attend the school they attended. Loyalty to alma mater intense enough to lead people to want to send their children there is obviously not an important factor among recent alumni.

Nor does there seem to be much romanticism about the advantages of the small college (Table 54). Only a quarter of the respondents think that a college under 2,000 is desirable for their oldest son, and only a third think it would be desirable for their oldest daughter. Thirty-nine percent of the respondents think a college of over 5,000 in size would be desirable for their son, and 32 percent think that a college of that size would be desirable for their daughter. The alumni clearly, then, accept the idea that the larger institution will become typical in American higher education, if indeed it has not already done so.

We have already indicated that general education, career training, personality development, and personal freedom were the most important criteria used by the alumni in choosing a college for their children. In Table 55 we list, in the order of their importance, all the possible choices of desirable college characteristics for one's offspring. The numbers in this table are gamma coefficients; that is, they demonstrate the strength of the relationship between a given variable and the desirability of a college characteristic. Thus the $-.14$ coefficient between sex and "college close to home" means that men are less likely than women to want to see their children in a college close to home, and the $-.20$ coefficient between "college close to home" and the private control of the college means that those who went to private colleges were less likely than those who went to public colleges to want to see their children in a college close to home. Men, on the other hand, are more likely to endorse personal freedom and an athletic program. General education and personal freedom are the favorites of the young, while all the other characteristics appeal to the older alumni. None of the relations with age is very strong.

Those who went to large colleges or high-quality colleges are not interested in religious education or personality development. Those from large colleges are less likely to endorse general education, and those from high-quality colleges are less likely to endorse career training, but there is no correlation between college quality and general education nor between size and career training. Personal freedom is substantially more important to those from high-quality colleges, and the college's being close to home is much less important to them. Finally, those from higher-quality colleges are not as much concerned with social class as are those who went to lower-quality colleges.

Graduates of private colleges are more likely than those who went to public colleges and universities to endorse general education and less likely to endorse career training; more likely to be in favor of personality development, religious education, and their own alma mater and less likely to be concerned both with fraternities and sororities and the school being close to home.

Those alumni who had the best grades in college reject athletic programs, Greek organizations, and alma mater. They are somewhat more likely than others to want a good general education. With the exception of athletic programs, none of these relations is

TABLE 55 *Coefficients of* *association* *between college* *characteristics* *desirable for* *oldest child of* *same sex as* *respondent* *and background* *variables* *(Gamma)*	

College characteristics	Sex (male)
The college offers a good general education	—.29
The college gives good career training	—.22
The faculty and administration are concerned with students' personality development	—.11
The college gives students a lot of personal freedom	.14
The college gives a good religious education	—.09
Students can join fraternities or sororities	.17
The college is close to home	—.14
There is an extensive athletic program at the college	.25
The college has students who are of the same social background as my child	—.09
It is the same college I graduated from	.04

strong. Even so, the fact that alumni who did well in school are the ones least likely to want to send their children to their alma mater should be cause for little rejoicing for their own college.

Some of the coefficients in Table 55 are large enough to be of some interest. General education is the favorite goal of higher education for the alumni, but especially if they were women, were younger, went to smaller or private colleges, or had good grades. Career training is also likely to be endorsed by women, by the older, by those who went to lower-quality or public colleges, or by those who got poor marks. Personality development, the third most important characteristic in choosing a college for one's children, is approved more by women than by men, more by those from small or private colleges than by those from large or public ones; but also it gets a stronger vote from those in lower-quality colleges, thus in this respect its support is different from the support for general education. Personal freedom, the fourth most important characteristic in choosing a school for one's offspring, on the other hand, has an entirely different pattern of support. Men, the younger alumni, graduates of high-quality colleges, and those who went to

| | | Background variables | | |
Age	College quality	College size	Private college	College grades
—.10	.01	—.12	.18	.10
.08	—.28	.04	—.31	—.08
.02	—.14	—. 15	.11	—.08
—.12	.22	.05	.08	.07
.03	—.18	—.21	.15	—.10
.05	—.11	.12	—.17	—.15
.15	—.24	.02	—.20	—.01
.04	—.05	.00	.00	—.26
.07	—.20	—.07	—.11	—.10
.02	.11	—.01	.09	—.15

private colleges are most likely to look for such personal freedom in a school for their children.

It is worth remarking that those who find it desirable for their children to attend a college in which there is a lot of personal freedom are quite consistent in advocating greater freedom for students at the present time (Table 56). Those who think that personal freedom is "very desirable" for their children all tend to score very high on the four indices of student involvement. As a matter of fact, there is a strong direct relationship between the desire for personal freedom for one's children and support of present student demands.

The alumni seek for their children, then, those characteristics that they found most important in their own college experience — general education, preparation for a career, opportunity to develop their personality, and the freedom to be themselves. The amount of emphasis they place on these four goals is affected to some extent by a number of background variables, but in particular by sex and by the quality and control of the college that they attended. However, the least important characteristic for them in choosing a school for their children is that it be their own alma mater. As we

TABLE 56 *Importance of personal freedom as characteristic of college for oldest child of same sex as respondent and student-involvement indices (Percent in highest quartile)*

Personal freedom in college for oldest child	Student- politics index	Rules index	Student- power index	Student- freedom index
Very desirable	63 (891)	40 (896)	38 (901)	66 (896)
Somewhat desirable	32 (3,096)	18 (3,128)	23 (3,124)	31 (3,081)
Neither	17 (1,817)	12 (1,831)	16 (1,821)	15 (1,795)
Somewhat undesirable	12 (1,517)	11 (1,511)	12 (1,512)	8 (1,477)
Very undesirable	7 (216)	8 (226)	17 (225)	2 (224)

noted above, it is those who got the poorer grades who are more likely to want their children to attend their alma mater—hardly an overwhelming vote of confidence.

THE ALUMNI SPEAK FOR THEMSELVES The concerns the alumni express in their own words are not substantively different from those presented more abstractly by the statistical tables—general education, career training, student unrest, personality development, and improvement of faculty. Some of the alumni provide rather detailed recommendations in response to the open-ended question on what changes they "would like to see in American higher education in the next ten years."

One young woman who teaches on a university faculty offered the following suggestions:

1. Less emphasis on research on the part of the faculty and more on *teaching,* most especially at the undergraduate level.

2. A chronological and coordinated approach to the social, political, economic, cultural development of man from the beginning of time, rather than disparate "requirements" to fill.

3. Smaller and more student-participation classes, rather than huge lectures—also more faculty-student consultation on *all* aspects of education.

4. Abolishment of the "in loco parentis" concept.

5. College should be a lower-class phenomenon for those qualified, not just something that the middle and upper classes do naturally upon graduation from High School. In other words remove financial barriers and un-

fairly determined measures of intelligence so that just about anyone can at least have a hack at it, as in California with their free Junior College system, where a high school diploma is not an absolute prerequisite.

A press agent in New York City made these recommendations:

I would like to see a large percentage of the supercharged intellectual professors and their abstractions eliminated from college and replaced by guys who can talk to students on the gut level and tell them what life is really about. Throw out the Mickey Mouse courses and the rote memory courses and instead start teaching what it is to be a human being, a father, a worker, a citizen, a husband, etc. Talk about birth, life and death. Talk about realities like poverty and prejudice, hatred and passion. Let's graduate kids who understand that life is more than J&B Scotch and playboy bunnies. Above all, teach them the meaning of love, because in the final analysis, that's all that's going to save this very, very sick world we live in.

A woman member of a faculty in a Catholic college demanded a profound change in the spirit of higher education:

A change in attitude or ways of thinking, something that will have to begin with the faculty and (hopefully) some enlightened administrators. We must redefine and understand the relevancy of higher education to 20th century society; we must understand the meaning of "service to the community"—a problem being faced by public institutions and some private; we must get away from the artificial distinction between "service school" and ivory tower *without* losing the understanding of *values* which has been part of higher education. Cf. Jencks and Riesman, *The Academic Revolution* [1968].

A mental health researcher also demanded drastic changes:

More outside lecturers should be brought in by an instructor—and these speakers should not necessarily be "expert"; they may be longshoremen, slum dwellers, poets, etc. Grades and exams should be relegated to the waste basket and students should have more say in determining course content. Defense contracts of any kind with a college or university should be permanently prohibited.

A housewife who did not attend graduate school summarized her reforms more briefly:

More attention paid to students as individuals and their growth as persons; more discussion of the world around them—day by day events (the campus can completely close out the *real* world); great deal more financial help to poor students and minority groups; grades could play a lesser role—they seem so childish now.

A married woman who describes herself only as "pretty happy," and who does research in a mental health institution, had the following thoughtful recommendations:

1. Techniques to increase social consciousness, self-understanding and combat some of the myths we were raised with—i.e., bigotry.
2. Work and study alternation programs to provide more meaningful experiences for students so they graduate more knowledgeable. These programs could relieve students' and parents' monetary burden also. They might probably be most useful in the last two years of college and would add only 1 more year to the time needed to get a bachelor's degree.
3. Increase use of TV to expose students to some really great lecturers and ideas. Example—use material from SUNY [State University of New York] and NET [National Educational Television] and supplement these with small discussion groups. This would save money too.

A male college English instructor, who observed that he doubted that he ever would contribute a dime to his alma mater, had the following observations:

1. Drop all education courses—worthless.
2. Hire people as teachers—not cripples.
3. Get rid of "publish or perish" or have teachers and scholars and not have them *have* to be both.
4. Drop as many controls as possible.
5. Have all teachers stop "teaching" and start learning, open up, drop fears, etc. No one should *teach* another.

And a female college teacher agreed with the emphasis on personality development:

I would like to see [American higher education] financed by a broader base and with more support from the public and state legislature.

I would like to see more emphasis on personal development, concern for others, understanding the world conditions and less on professional and scientific education.

I would like to see college faculties and administrators be more concerned for students and not so self-centered.

The theme of improvement of the faculty runs through many of the comments. A male alumnus said: "Removal of the teachers that are totally out of touch with the reality of life. You'll have to excuse the last statement—I see too many teachers." An Army officer observed: "The hiring of faculty members on their ability to teach and/or stimulate the student—not on their (faculty's) knowledge of subject without regard to ability to communicate!!"

Many of the alumni were quite upset with student unrest. A male observed: "Discipline restored to campuses. Make it clear that students come to college and if they do not like things they can get out." And another male said: "Students should have less control on administration." A female contemporary remarked: "I see one thing that is happening that I don't like and that is that the students are gaining too much control over the schools." An Army officer noted: "I should like to see universities take a firm hand in dealing with dissidents. Students must be taught respect for law and order and any radical variance will not be tolerated. Academic freedom is great, but things have gotten out of hand." And an Irish policeman echoed his military counterpart's feelings: "Schools should take the initiative in stopping student take-overs. This is *ridiculous*. If they don't like school get out."

Among others, a surgeon asked for the following three changes:

1. Greater screening of college applicants to eliminate undesirables.
2. A firmer stand against groups who advocate violence, sit-in, riot, pick-it for the sake of "something to do."
3. Again further *encouragement* of *in*-state enrollment and further *discouragement* of *out*-of-state enrollment.

Some of the alumni, however, took a more benign view of student unrest. One young man said: "This *in loco parentis* attitude of many of our college and university administrations is appalling. It's the old argument—if you are old enough to be drafted (18–19) or in college you should be allowed to vote, drink, make your own decisions, etc."

Some of the respondents emphasized strongly the vocational aspects of higher education. A housewife from New York observed:

Courses should stress more practical application instead of theory. Most of the courses I took were too theory-oriented. Also higher education should try to prepare the graduate for the "outside world." . . . The academic world is an entity in itself. Many graduates I have talked with have found they aren't emotionally or academically prepared for everyday life away from the campus.

A housewife in Maryland concluded: "Stricter and more emphasis on career and discipline training."

But a larger proportion of the alumni stressed the opposite point. A clergyman from Indiana said:

Even in the face of the apparent need for greater specialization, I feel a real need for more emphasis on general education. The increase of highly trained, uneducated persons is sad — and unwholesome for a powerful democratic republic.

A housewife-computer programmer from Massachusetts said:

Higher education should provide greater variety and scope of fields, with better opportunity for the students to try out those fields that interest them. Less emphasis on career training in colleges with more specifically career-oriented junior colleges or trade schools. Less emphasis on grades and formal classwork, more independent study and contact with the faculty.

However, the most frequently mentioned recommendation from the alumni concerns the broad area of personality and character development. A Long Island housewife said:

More emphasis needs to be placed on developing the *whole* personality, not just the brain. I graduated *cum laude,* but I still think our society needs people who care about one another, not just people who know statistics, dates, and all the angles.

A Chicago housewife who also is a Russian translator observed: "I'd like to see American higher education provide all U.S. high school graduates with a set of opportunities to become responsible adults of good conscience. That's the ideal!"

An Army personnel psychologist noted:

If the value of a college education is to endure, both students and faculty and administration must recognize that the university cannot meet, solve, and absolve all the problems of our complex society. The university must define its role, place emphasis on preparing young people for making positive contributions in the world outside the ivy covered walls. "Publish or perish," drinking on campus, the Rose Bowl winner—these trivia pale when one views the real challenges facing the future college graduates.

An M.D. from Rochester observed:

I would like to see more emphasis at the undergraduate level on the development of character, integrity, and the ability to interact with society; more freedom to pursue one's own interests and long term goals, and more stress made on one's ability to think objectively and independently.

And finally, a housewife from Montana said:

I would like to see colleges prepare students not only for a career, but also give them a greater understanding of others, with a greater understanding and toleration for others' ideas. This is perhaps slowly coming about. Instead of the instructors feeding information to students, help them to reach this understanding themselves. Then they will be prepared not only for careers, but for life in a changing, growing society.

The grammar and rhetoric of the alumni's hastily written comments may not be flawless, but their concern about American society and their desire that higher education prepare young people for responsible behavior in that society come through loud and clear. Very few of the suggestions are at odds with the traditions of American higher education. Educators will perhaps lament the fact that the respondents do not really seem to understand how difficult it is to achieve the goals they describe.

One might summarize the alumni suggestions for the reform of higher education under the following headings:

1 They are concerned with the "real world" and how it might be improved.

2 They view themselves as "citizens" of the real world and they are concerned with how higher education might better enable them to participate as citizens in the real world.

3 As socially responsible citizens of the real world, the alumni emphasize the obligation of higher education to prepare them and their successors for responsible participation in resolving the *social problems* of the real world.

Thus the themes of social problems, responsibility, participation, and reality run through not only the statistical data reported in this chapter, but also through the responses the alumni have delivered in their own words. They may differ in rhetoric from their successors on the college campus—our respondents are far "cooler" than the younger generation. They may also differ in their views on how people might be trained for responsible social participation; they are much less likely to approve various aspects of student power than the present generation seems to be, and even among themselves there is a generation gap. Nevertheless, while the style of protest and even the substance of some of the demands for reform seem to be different, the basic ideal that a college should train its graduates for responsible adult social participation did not come into existence within the last three or four years. In their own way, the alumni of 1961 endorsed this goal too. Even though they, like other Americans, may be overly optimistic about the extent to which higher education can by itself successfully train people for responsible adult social participation, there is not much doubt that they expect the colleges to exercise substantial effort toward the achievement of such a goal.

SUMMARY   Only the most naive reformer would argue that the wishes of the young alumni should be decisive for higher education. Yet their suggestions, explicit and implicit, for reform have some right to be taken seriously. The 1961 alumni are close enough to their higher educational experience to have some fairly clear memory of what it was like and far enough into their postgraduate lives to be able to evaluate their higher education against the background of their lives.

1   When asked what they would do differently, the alumni overwhelmingly choose courses and express interests in the arts and sciences, especially in the humanities, and most especially in the fine arts.

2   It is precisely those whose careers were such that little specific career preparation was possible in college who are the most likely to display such humanistic inclinations. Those such as engineers, educators, or businessmen, for whom rather specific undergraduate career training was possible, seem much less humanistic in their actions than do the others. Nonetheless, even this group shows reasonably strong humanistic orientations.

3 There is some sympathy for student involvement, but it is highly selective. The alumni are not willing to give students power on questions of tenure, admission standards, tuition, or what is taught in specific courses, but they are willing to concede to the students a role in the organization of the curriculum, in the *enforcement* of rules, and in the participation of students in off-campus activities.

4 Sympathy for student involvement is to be found more in women than in men, more in younger alumni than in older, and more in graduates of high-quality colleges than in graduates of low-quality colleges.

5 The alumni are also in sympathy with the possibility of moratoriums both between high school and college and during college, and they strongly support college education for women as essential to their role as wife and mother.

6 The most important characteristic in choosing a college for their own children is that the college provide a good general education; the second most important characteristic is career training. They do not view career training and general education as mutually exclusive. Personality development and personal freedom are the other two characteristics that receive strong support as being desirable in a college for their children.

7 The general-education goal in college for one's children is more important for women than for men, for young alumni than for old, and for the graduates of private colleges than for the graduates of public colleges. On the other hand, career training as a goal, while also more important for women than for men, is more important for the older rather than for the younger alumni, and for the graduates of lower-quality colleges and public colleges.

8 The least important characteristic in choosing a college for one's children is that it be one's own college. The only coefficients above .1 on this item are $-.15$ for college grades and .11 for college quality. In other words, it is precisely those students who got the poorest marks who are most likely to want their children to attend their alma mater—but even they are not very likely to want it.

CONCLUSION What reforms for higher education are the alumni advocating explicitly and implicitly in their responses to our questions? A number of points are fairly evident:

1   If they are forced to choose between being vocationalists or generalists, the alumni lean heavily on the side of generalism. *But* it is also clear that considerable numbers of them are generalists because they view general education as the best, or at least the only possible, kind of career preparation they can receive in college.

2   Within the general-education tradition, the liberal arts (including the social sciences) are more popular than the physical sciences with the alumni; and within the liberal arts, the humanities and especially the fine arts are the most popular. Thus, we would conclude that the alumni are endorsing more general education, more concern for the humanities, and especially more concern for the fine arts.

3   Alumni are willing to permit student involvement in curriculum formation and enforcement of rules, and support free political activity off campus, though more than four-fifths are opposed to student involvement in such matters as tenure, admissions, and tuition. And around three-fifths think that the college should regulate students and that students have no right to make decisions about what is taught in specific courses. Approximately half think that the college has the responsibility of seeing that students do not break the law, are opposed to the right to protest against campus recruiters, and think that the college should act *in loco parentis* and that students do not have the right to participate in the *making* of rules. If half think this way, it is likely that half think the opposite way, so on matters of rule making and rule enforcement, educators receive mixed advice from the alumni. The most radical demands of the student protesters are rejected, the mildest demands are accepted, and demands about rule making and law enforcing produce decidedly mixed reactions.

4   When given a chance to express their own feelings on these matters in their own words, the alumni generally are strongly in favor of more of those aspects of education that educators themselves have traditionally endorsed as being central to the higher educational concern. As one Montana housewife said:

> I would like to see colleges prepare students not only for a career, but also give them a greater understanding of others. . . . [Instructors should] help them to reach this understanding themselves. Then they will be prepared not only for careers, but for life in a changing, growing society.

The data reported in this chapter could be used either to support or to oppose demands for major higher educational reform, and particularly for greater student involvement in the decision-making process. The alumni seem evenly divided on the issues of student power, and while they are very enthusiastic for humanistic education, they also expect to be trained for their careers. It is worth noting, however, that these representatives of the supposedly apathetic generation are espousing values and goals that are not strikingly different from those of their more radical successors. The style may be somewhat different, and even certain specific reforms do not win as much enthusiasm among the alumni as they do among present undergraduates. Nevertheless, very substantial segments of the alumni population seem to want from higher education exactly the same kinds of things that their more outspoken younger brothers and sisters are demanding. Curiously enough, both groups frequently seem to be asking for exactly what the college catalogs have promised. If higher educational institutions are being criticized, they are being criticized in terms of their own values — which, in its own way, is both a compliment and a tribute as well as something of a threat.

Educators will probably find themselves ambivalent in their reactions to this chapter. In their strong endorsement of humanistic concerns, their cautious moderation regarding student protest, and their emphasis on training for responsible adult behavior, the alumni seem not only to be endorsing higher educational reforms that would enable higher education to live up to the best of its own presumed goals, but their personal reactions frequently sound like repetitions of what they read in college catalogs. But educators may also feel that the alumni are implying that such humanistic, moderate, responsible goals could be achieved in a far more effective fashion than they have, in fact, been achieved thus far. The reluctance of the alumni to think it "very desirable" or even "somewhat desirable" that their children attend their own school, while in part perhaps attributable to a respect for their offsprings' freedom of choice, also suggests a lack of enthusiasm for their own higher educational experience, which many educators may perhaps find disturbing.

6. Political and Social Attitudes

The June, 1961 alumni graduated from college just as the volunteer or the protest movements began, but were not so old that they would not be affected by these movements. As Table 57 demonstrates, only 4 percent of the alumni have ever experimented with drugs, 5 percent have participated in antiwar protests, 2 percent have worked full time for a service organization, and 9 percent have participated in civil rights protests. However, 43 percent have engaged in some kind of volunteer activity, and almost all (91 percent) would approve if their children engaged in such an activity. Nearly three-fourths would support formal volunteer service for their children, about one-third would support civil rights protests, and 15 percent would approve of antiwar protests by their children. Thus, the June, 1961 graduates are well disposed toward volunteering, but unsympathetic toward protests both in their own behavior and in their children's.

PARTY AFFILIATION AND POLITICAL ORIENTATION There is also not much trace of radicalism in their political self-description. In Tables 58 and 59 we trace changing party affiliations of the 1961 alumni by comparing the affiliation of their parents with that of the alumni in both 1964 and 1968. Approximately the same proportion (43 percent) reported themselves as Republican in 1968 as came from Republican families (44 percent). However, Democratic affiliation declined dramatically from 44 percent in the parental generation to 29 percent in the respondent generation. All the loss of the Democrats was to the benefit of the Independents, who composed more than one-quarter of the alumni in 1968 and only 8 percent of the parental generation.

However, there were interesting shifts between 1964 and 1968, with an upswing for the Republicans of 5 percent and a downswing for the Democrats of 7 percent. Thus the Republican curve at the

TABLE 57
Alumni attitudes on certain experiences (Percent)

Experiences	I have	I would approve if one of my children
Experimented with drugs	4	1
Participated in an antiwar protest	5	15
Participated in civil rights protest	9	30
Worked full time for a service organization such as the Peace Corps, VISTA, or the American Friends Service Committee	2	73
Volunteered to help others (a project to tutor under-privileged students, helping in a mental hospital, etc.)	43	91

three time periods from parents to 1968 is U-shaped, but the Democratic curve is a downward slant and the Independent curve an upward slant. To what extent the confused, frustrating, and bitter 1968 Presidential campaign contributed to this change remains to be seen. The data for the study were collected after President Johnson's withdrawal and before the assassination of Senator Robert Kennedy.

The bottom part of Table 58 shows that while the alumni are considerably more likely to describe themselves as political liberals

TABLE 58
Party affiliation and political orientation of alumni and their parents (Percent)

Affiliation	Parents	Alumni 1964	Alumni 1968
Party affiliation:			
Republican	44	38	43
Democratic	44	36	29
Independent	8	24	26
Other	3	2	2
TOTAL	99	100	100
Political orientation:			
Liberal	40	56	52

than they are to describe their parents as such, nonetheless there has been a decrease (4 percentage points) of liberalism and a corresponding increase of conservatism since 1964.

Table 59 indicates that when party affiliation and political orientation are combined, the principal losers between 1964 and 1968 are the liberal Democrats, and the principal gainers are the conservative Republicans. Liberalism is able to more or less hold its own, but the Democratic party is not. The strength of the trend away from the Democrats in 1968 is shown in Table 60, in which not only the respondent's party affiliation in 1964 and 1968 is considered, but also the party affiliation of the respondent's parents. The Democratic party has not been able to attract back into the fold more than a handful of those children of Democratic families who had become Republicans or Independents by 1964, and, on the contrary, has lost more than one-quarter of those who were Democrats in 1964. The principal gainers, however, from the Democratic defections are the so-called Independents, and not the Republicans.

The Republicans, on the other hand, have been able to retain almost nine-tenths of those whose parents were Republicans and were themselves Republicans in 1964 and to attract back 22 percent of those from Republican backgrounds who were Democrats in 1964 and 39 percent of those who were Independents in 1964. Finally, the Republicans have made strong inroads into the ranks of those who came from Independent family backgrounds and even into the ranks of those whose backgrounds were Independent and who themselves were Independent in 1964 (32 percent).

Changes		Net change
Parent to 1964	*1964 to 1968*	*Parent to 1968*
−6	+5	−1
−8	−7	−15
+16	+2	+18
−1	0	−1
+16	−4	+12

TABLE 59
*Political leanings
of alumni, 1964
and 1968
(Percent)*

Political leaning	1964	1968	Net difference
Conservative Republican	18	22	+4
Liberal Republican	20	21	+1
Conservative Democrat	13	12	−1
Liberal Democrat	23	18	−5
Conservative Independent	11	12	+1
Liberal Independent	13	14	+1
New Left	–	1	+1
Other	2	1	−1

One might have expected that the capacity of a given party to retain its membership in the years between 1964 and 1968 might be a function of income — the Democrats most likely to lose among well-to-do alumni and the Republicans most likely to lose among not-so-well-to-do alumni. However, Table 61 shows that class differences do not, in fact, seem to relate, at least at this age in life, to party loyalties. The Republican, Democratic, and Independent parties show little variation across income lines in their capacity to retain those who were affiliated with them in 1964.

Perhaps the erosion of Democratic strength indicated in Tables 58 through 61 is part of the natural change in the economic and social perspective of the college alumni or is related specifically to the confusing political situation of 1968. In any event, the changes between liberal and conservative orientation do not seem to be very striking when the political orientation of parents is held con-

TABLE 60
*1968 party
affiliation by
1964 party
affiliation and
parental party
affiliation
(Percent)*

1968 party affiliation	Republican		
	1964 party affiliation		
	Republican	Democratic	Independent
Republican	85	22	39
Democratic	4	53	8
Independent	11	26	54
N	(2,072)	(446)	(686)

stant (Table 62). Thus, the "liberalization" of college students reported by Spaeth (forthcoming, Chapter 3) and others does not seem to have been affected either by the passage of time or by the political events of 1968. The Democratic party has lost strength, but more of it to Independents than to Republicans, though the Republicans have made gains; but there has been only a minor erosion of liberalism.

**ATTITUDES
TOWARD
CURRENT
ISSUES**

The basic split in the alumni—half liberal and half conservative—affects their reaction to current political issues (Table 63). Approximately half of them were in sympathy with college protests, and half thought the country would be better off if there were less protest and dissatisfaction. Two-fifths thought the protesters should lose their draft deferments, but two-thirds thought that both undergraduate and graduate students should get deferments. A little more than half thought that in the long run the Negro protests would be healthy for America, but two-thirds thought that Negro militancy was needlessly dividing America, and only 36 percent were willing to admit the advocacy in the conclusion of the Kerner report that the main cause of Negro riots in the cities is white racism.

When the alumni are compared with their parents, one can say that a college education produces substantial gains for both liberals and Independents, substantial losses for Democrats, and with Republicans "breaking even." But the critical question is: What do these shifts mean in terms of concrete political issues? Is a liberal Republican more "liberal" than a liberal Democrat? Is a conservative Independent more "conservative" than a conservative Republican? Table 64 enables us to provide answers to these questions

Parental party affiliation					
Democratic			Independent		
1964 party affiliation			1964 party affiliation		
Republican	Democratic	Independent	Republican	Democratic	Independent
74	9	21	63	18	32
8	73	20	2	58	14
17	18	58	35	25	54
(577)	(1,894)	(663)	(161)	(163)	(376)

TABLE 61
Retention of party affiliation between 1964 and 1968, by present family income

Present family income	Party affiliation		
	Republican	Democratic	Independent
$15,000 and over	81	66	53
$11,000–$14,000	84	66	54
$8,000–$10,000	79	68	50
Under $8,000	77	65	63

TABLE 62
1968 political orientation by 1964 political orientation and parental political orientation (Percent)

1968 political orientation	Parental political orientation			
	Conservative		Liberal	
	1964 political orientation		1964 political orientation	
	Conservative	Liberal	Conservative	Liberal
Conservative	67	33	63	31
Liberal	33	67	37	69
N	(2,198)	(2,042)	(799)	(1,999)

TABLE 63
Alumni attitudes on current issues (Percent)

Statement	Agree strongly or somewhat
College students should get draft deferments	69
Negro militancy is needlessly dividing American society into conflicting camps	67
Graduate students should get draft deferments	63
In the long run, current protests of Negroes in the cities will be healthy for America	56
This country would be better off if there were less protest and dissatisfaction coming from college campuses	52
The protests of college students are a healthy sign for America	51
College students should lose their draft deferments for participating in demonstrations against the draft	42
The main cause of Negro riots in the cities is white racism	36

TABLE 64 *Attitudes on student and Negro protests, by political leanings (Percent agree strongly or somewhat)*

| | Political leaning | | | | | | |
| | Republican | | Democratic | | Independent | | |
Attitude	Conser-vative	Liberal	Conser-vative	Liberal	Conser-vative	Liberal	New Left
Student protests a healthy sign for America	30	55	36	64	43	77	97
Negro protests will be healthy for America	33	58	44	73	50	78	97
N	(1,638)	(1,595)	(899)	(1,292)	(914)	(1,031)	(89)

for the issues of student unrest and race. The striking finding in this table is that on both issues the Independents, whether they be conservative or liberal, are more "liberal" than their counterparts in either the Democratic or the Republican party. Liberal Independents are more "liberal" than liberal Democrats, who are, in their turn, more "liberal" than liberal Republicans. But in addition, conservative Independents are more "liberal" than conservative Democrats or Republicans and only somewhat less likely to be "liberal" than are liberal Republicans.

One therefore can argue that, at least for the June, 1961 college graduates, the trend toward being an Independent is a trend to the left in regard to the racial and student protest issues.

SUPPORT FOR MILITANCY At least half, then, of the alumni are willing to express at least moderate sympathy with both the black and student protesters, but only about a third are willing to take a strong stand endorsing the Kerner report, while two-thirds argue that protests needlessly divide America. Another half seem opposed to protests in whatever form. The reactions to black and student protests correlate highly enough that they can be combined in one index, *support for militancy,* which contains the following items:

- The protests of college students are a healthy sign for America. (Agree)
- This country would be better off if there were less protest and dissatisfaction coming from college campuses. (Disagree)
- In the long run, current protests of Negroes in the cities will be healthy for America. (Agree)

TABLE 65	

TABLE 65
Coefficients of
association
between
support-for-
militancy index
and selected
variables

Variable	Gamma
Background variable:	
College quality	.22
College size	.00
Control (private)	.17
College grades	.17
Years in graduate school	.27
Father's education	.15
Sex (male)	—.02
Age	—.18
Incidence of protests on campus, 1967–1968:	
Any	—.12
Moderately severe	—.13
Prolonged or repeated	—.15

- The main cause of Negro riots in the cities is white racism. (Agree)
- Negro militancy is needlessly dividing American society into conflicting camps. (Disagree)
- College students should lose their draft deferments for participating in demonstrations against the draft. (Disagree)

As Table 65 informs us, it is the alumni from good colleges and from private colleges, those with good grades, those who have spent several years in graduate school, those with upper-middle-class backgrounds, and those who are younger who are the most likely to be in sympathy with protests, both black and student. The correlations (.22, .17, and —.18) are substantial and presumably relatively independent of one another. Furthermore, they agree rather well with what we know from other research. It is the younger, more intelligent students of the high-quality colleges who are the most likely to protest. Similarly, it is their counterparts in the alumni generation who are most likely to be in sympathy with protests.

There are also moderate negative correlations (—.12, —.13, and —.15) between incidence of protests at one's own school in

TABLE 66
Support-for-militancy index by type of college attended

Type of college attended	Percent in highest quartile
University (large public)	24
University (private)	37
University (other)	28
Protestant (low quality)	18
Protestant (high quality)	34
State college	18
Catholic	28
Liberal arts college	34

1967–1968 and the support-for-militancy index.[1] While these gammas are sufficiently large to be worth noting, they do not indicate, as of spring, 1968, a powerful relationship between disruption at one's alma mater and unfavorable attitudes toward student or black protests in general. Given the fact that feelings toward the alma mater are not very intense in any case, one would not be too surprised that disruption in their school has relatively little effect on the attitudes of most alumni.

Because of the relationship between college quality and the score on the support-for-militancy index, we are not unprepared for the findings in Table 66 that the graduates of the private universities, the "high-quality" Protestant colleges, and the liberal arts colleges are the most likely to be in sympathy with protests and that the graduates of the state colleges and "low-quality" Protestant colleges are the least likely. Similarly, previous research prepares us for the data reported in Table 67, indicating that it is particularly those in the arts and sciences—especially the social scientists and the humanists—who are the most sympathetic to protests. What is quite surprising, however, is that lawyers are second only to social

[1] Data on the presence or absence of protests were gained through the courtesy of Richard Peterson of the Educational Testing Service. He carried out a survey of educational administrators that asked about the extent of protest on most of the campuses in the country. He very graciously allowed us to use his data on protests. Most of the colleges in our sample were classified according to Peterson's data on whether they had had politically related protests of any kind, of a moderately severe kind, or of a "prolonged or repeated" kind. For further details, see Peterson (1968).

TABLE 67
Support-for-militancy index by 1968 career field

1968 career field	Percent in highest quartile
Physical sciences	36
Biological sciences	33
Social sciences	54
Humanities	62
Engineering	14
Medicine	33
Other health	11
Education	24
Business	15
Law	48
Other professions	35

scientists and humanists in their support of protests. Perhaps the lawyer's concern with human rights and due process makes him sympathetic with the attempts of students and black groups to obtain such rights and processes in their own lives. Nonetheless, it is worth noting that the young lawyers seem to be taking a very liberal view on the issue of "law and order."

The multiple regression analysis done on the support-for-militancy index was successful in explaining 18 percent of the variance. The major explanatory variables were college quality, college grades, and number of years in graduate school, each of which independently explained approximately 3 percent of the variance. Other fairly helpful explanatory variables (that is, above 1 percent of the variance explained) were father's education, respondent's age, religion, and a choice of career in the humanities. The characteristics that other research has indicated as typical of the protesters are also typical of the supporters of the protesters among the present alumni.

The correlation between age and sympathy with protesters is extremely interesting because it must be remembered that all the alumni graduated from college at the same time. Nevertheless, even among the alumni, a generation gap exists. Table 68 indicates the striking dimensions of this generation gap. The alumni who are 28 or under and from the best colleges are more than four times as likely to score high on the support-for-militancy index as the alumni

TABLE 68
Support-for-
militancy index
by age and
college quality
(Percent in
highest
quartile)

	Age		
College quality	28 or younger	29–31	Over 31
High	44 (1,208)	35 (737)	28 (158)
Medium	30 (1,151)	23 (879)	21 (304)
Low	23 (1,366)	16 (1,097)	10 (661)

over 31 from the lowest-quality colleges. But even more strikingly, the alumni over 31 from the best colleges are only 5 percentage points more likely to score high on the support-for-militancy index than are the younger alumni (those 28 or under) from the poorest colleges. Furthermore, those between 29 and 31 at all three quality levels seem to be closer in attitude to those over 31 than they are to those who are 28 or younger. Table 68 would indicate not only that you cannot trust anyone over 30 but that you had better be suspicious of anyone over 29.

CONCLUSION As a body, the June, 1961 alumni can be described as "moderate," but leaning a bit to the left. Politically, the trend is toward being an Independent, a position that apparently represents a more liberal viewpoint than either the Republican or the Democratic party stands for. Consistently enough, our alumni are more likely to think of themselves as liberals than they are to describe their parents as liberals. About half of them are willing to give qualified support to militancy, be it black or student, but only a little more than a third are willing to endorse the Kerner report's conclusion about the origins of urban riots. Those who are in strongest sympathy with protests are the younger alumni and those who came from upper-middle-class backgrounds. They were likely to have attended a high-quality and private undergraduate institution, to have received good grades, and to have spent several years in graduate school. Humanists, social scientists, and lawyers are somewhat more favorably disposed to protesters than are alumni with other career interests. The generation gap is noteworthy; those 28 or younger (at the time the data were collected) were far more sympathetic to protest than were those 29 or over.

However, the fact that their own alma mater was the site of a disturbance seems to have relatively small effect on alumni reaction, at least in the spring of 1968. The 1961 alumni do not dramatically and vigorously reject the protests of their younger brothers and sisters; neither do they very powerfully endorse them. One wonders what the 1969 alumni will think seven years hence.

7. Financial Contributions to Alma Mater

No college can rely solely on its alumni for the funding necessary to keep going. As we noted in Chapter 1, the class of '61 made a financial contribution whose magnitude is quite slight in comparison with the needs of American higher education. In 1967–68, 37 percent made a contribution; the mean gift was about $10. Two percent of the sample gave $100 or over, 5 percent gave $50 or more, and 15 percent gave at least $20.

It has been argued, however, that the magnitude is less important than the proportion making a contribution. When they approach potential donors of large gifts, college fund raisers use the rate of alumni giving as indicative of the extent of loyalty to alma mater and thus of the institution's worthiness for further support. From that point of view, anything that raises or lowers the percentage of alumni making a contribution may have a pronounced effect on an institution's ability to raise rather large amounts of money.

We must certainly wonder about the relation between campus protests and alumni financial support. Big gifts have apparently declined at colleges that have experienced newsworthy protests. What about the giving of this group of relatively recent alumni? As Chapter 6 showed, the class of '61 is about evenly split in its views of militant campus dissent. Will the half that view it with disfavor tend to decrease their giving in the future? If so, colleges could be in for financial difficulties even greater than those they are now suffering or even greater than those they had earlier expected to meet.

CORRELATES OF GIVING A person's willingness to contribute financially to his alma mater will be governed by many factors other than campus dissent. These may include loyalty to one's college, the feeling that it contributed

TABLE 69
Coefficients of association between amount of financial contribution to alma mater "during the past 12 months" and selected variables

Variable	Gamma
Amount of contribution planned for "the next 12 months"	.85
Control (private)	.49
Emotional attachment to college in 1968	.33
Desirable to send children to alma mater	.27
College quality (Astin index)	.25
Number of colleges attended	—.23
College preparation for graduate school	.22
Parental SES (socioeconomic status)	.22
Perceived quality of college	.21
Parental family income	.20
Father's education	.18
Emotional attachment to college in 1961	.17
College size	—.15
Present family income	.14
Age	—.12
Criticism of college	—.10
Support for militancy	.09
Incidence of protests on campus, 1967–1968:*	
Any	.01
Moderately severe	—.04
Prolonged or repeated	—.01

*Correlations are with planning to contribute during the next 12 months.

to one's development, the type of college attended, and the perspective from which it is viewed.

Table 69 lists a series of items covering matters of the kind just mentioned, ranging from such basic facts about the institution as its size and control to the presence or absence of protest. The entries in the table are gammas, which indicate the amount of relationship between the variable and the making of a contribution to alma mater "during the past 12 months." The items are ordered from the strongest correlate to the weakest.

The first item is whether the person planned to make a contribution "during the next 12 months." The gamma between giving in one year and planning to give in the next is .85. Nearly all the people who gave something to their college planned to give again;

practically none of those who failed to make a contribution expected to make one the following year. Among the people who gave, 92 percent said they would give again; among those who did not give, only 13 percent said that they planned to do so. This finding implies that there is little relation between campus protest and alumni giving. Later, we shall look at this matter more closely.

Even though the chances of persuading a nongiver to become a giver seem rather slight, the rate of giving will increase from 37 to 42 percent—if the alumni do as they say they will. One reason for this increase is that there are more nongivers than givers. Gaining 13 percent of the former and losing only 8 percent of the latter results in a substantial net increase in the proportion who will contribute. Such a projection may be somewhat optimistic, of course. It seems likely that the actual deed will not always follow the good intentions.

The second strongest correlate of alumni giving is a characteristic of alma mater, control. The gamma of .49 indicates that graduates of private colleges were considerably more likely than graduates of public ones to make a gift. Further down the list, we find another institutional characteristic that is strongly related to giving. The graduates of the better colleges were more likely to contribute than those of the poorer colleges, as the gamma of .25 shows.

The relation between college size and giving is —.15, a rather small value. Though alumni of smaller, presumably more intimate, colleges were more likely to be contributors, large size is not in itself an insurmountable obstacle to gaining alumni financial support.

The relation between college characteristics and contributions suggests that alumni reactions to their college may also be related to their financial generosity. The third largest association in Table 69 involves just such an item. Persons who said in 1968 that they were emotionally attached to their college were more likely than others to make a contribution, as the gamma of .33 indicates.

Note that responses to the same question asked in 1961, when respondents were seniors, are much less closely related to the making of a gift. Whatever happened in the seven years after graduation that altered a person's attachment to his college also affected the likelihood that he would make a financial contribution to it.

The number of colleges attended can also be construed as an indicator of alumni loyalty. The gamma of —.23 indicates that persons who had attended only one college were more likely to make a contribution than those who had attended several. Conflicting loyalties may have something to do with this. In addition, persons who had attended more than one college were quite likely to have taken longer than the normal four years to graduate. The college from which they ultimately graduated may have been chosen for convenience in combining school with work or raising a family. If so, alumni of such institutions would have had little opportunity to become integrated into a campus culture and might therefore have formed little attachment to their last college.

It is worth noting that being critical of one's alma mater is not strongly related to making a gift or failing to do so. The gamma of —.10 shows that people with criticisms are somewhat less likely to contribute but not very much so.

In addition to characteristics of the college and the alumni's loyalty to it, a third set of items related to contributions concerns the persons' life histories. If they came from relatively affluent families, they were more likely to contribute than if they did not. The gamma between parental family income and contributing is .20; that for father's education is .18. Parental socioeconomic status (SES), which is an index based on the two variables just mentioned plus father's occupation, has a gamma of .22.

It should be noted that the income of the family in which the person grew up is more closely related to giving than are his own present financial resources. The gamma between present family income and contributing is only .14. This rather moderate value indicates that current financial resources are not much of a limitation on a person's generosity to his college, a fact that can be true only because of the smallness of the contributions involved.

The relation between parental characteristics and giving may be a clue pointing to the existence of a rather amorphous set of expectations having to do with giving to one's college—perhaps with charitable giving in general. From this point of view, the behavior of parents might serve as a model for that of their children. The better-educated and more affluent parents were doubtless more likely to make such contributions than those who were less well off.

Consistent with this idea is the relation between control and giving to one's college. Graduates of private colleges have traditionally included the monetary as part of their obligations to their colleges. This practice may be almost a matter of course in some of the elite colleges, and it may be a matter of rather explicit obligation in some of the religious ones. It has apparently not been part of the tacit obligations of public college alumni.

What about the effects of campus dissent on alumni giving? In spring, 1968, they were essentially nil. It is true that alumni who supported the militants were a little more likely to make a contribution, but the presence or absence of protests on campus was not related to giving. The gamma between the occurrence of prolonged or repeated protests on campus and anticipated contributions is —.01. (The protest items were correlated with intentions for next year so that contributions made prior to a protest would not artificially deflate the relationship.)

The three most important kinds of variables related to alumni giving are characteristics of the college, the person's loyalty to it, and his family background. It is not possible to compute gamma for the classification of college type used earlier in this report, but Table 70, which gives the percentage making a contribution among alumni of each type of institution, bears out the importance of college characteristics. Alumni of independent liberal arts colleges were most likely to make a contribution (68 percent), and alumni of state colleges were least likely to do so (17 percent). The two kinds of public institutions are at the bottom of the list, and, except for the "low-quality" Protestant colleges, the private colleges seem able to count on contributions from at least half of their 1961 alumni.

These findings are consistent with earlier ones regarding control and college quality. The operations of both variables can be discerned in the ordering of college types in Table 70. Even though quality and control do not explain the entire impact of college type (as determined by a table not shown here), the remainder of this

TABLE 70 *Having contributed to alma mater by type of college attended*		

Type of college attended	Percent	N
Liberal arts college	68	295
Protestant (high quality)	54	964
University (private)	50	843
Catholic	47	856
Protestant (low quality)	36	629
University (public)*	29	1,243
State college	17	1,396

*Includes miscellaneous universities.

TABLE 71
Percent who
contributed to
alma mater,
by college
control and
college quality

College quality	Control	
	Private	Public
High	68	–
	(345)	(0)
	58	27
	(473)	(179)
	43	31
	(842)	(324)
	54	26
	(1,167)	(1,226)
	45	27
	(532)	(703)
	40	18
	(508)	(802)
Low	32	13
	(187)	(528)

chapter will deal with these two characteristics. In that way, we shall have enough cases to examine the impact of other factors that we have already shown to be related to the making of a contribution.

Henceforth we shall be looking at the percentage of respondents who made a contribution of any amount at all. The small size of alumni gifts and the use of this figure as symbolic of loyalty by alumni officers make this procedure an appropriate one.

SOME DETERMINANTS OF GIVING

Table 71 shows the joint influence of control and quality on the making of a financial contribution. In the first column of the table are figures for the graduates of private institutions. The lowest percentage in this column is higher than any in the second column, which pertains to public college alumni. In other words, even the lowest-quality private institutions were at least as able to garner alumni support as the best public ones. Furthermore, college quality is much more highly related to financial support among alumni of private colleges than among those of public colleges. In the former, the percentage contributing ranges from 68 to 32. In the latter, only institutions in the two lowest-quality levels fall much below the general rate of 26 to 31 percent.

Could loyalty to alma mater be one reason why private college alumni were more likely to contribute than public college alumni? Could loyalty explain why graduates from the better private col-

	Emotional attachment to college	
Control	*Strong*	*Not strong*
Private	63	44
	(1,178)	(2,842)
Public	38	19
	(877)	(2,814)

TABLE 72 *Percent who contributed to alma mater, by emotional attachment to college and college control*

leges were more likely to make a contribution than those from the poorer ones? Table 72 gives the relationship between alumni contributions, control, and emotional attachment to one's college. It shows that each variable acts independently of the others and adds substantially to the explanation of alumni giving. If they were strongly attached to alma mater, graduates of private colleges were 25 percentage points more likely to make a contribution than those from public colleges; the same is true of alumni whose attachment was weaker. Among private college alumni, someone with strong emotional attachment was 19 percentage points more likely to make a contribution than someone with lesser attachment; the same is true of public college alumni. Emotional attachment does not explain why private college graduates are more likely to contribute than public college graduates. Both emotional attachment and control need to be taken into consideration.

What about college quality? Table 73 indicates that the relationship between quality and contribution depends on a person's emotional attachment. If someone was strongly attached to his college, he was much more likely to contribute to it if it was a good one than if it was a poor one. The percentages run from 65 for the high-quality colleges to 37 for the low-quality ones. Among alumni with weaker attachments, giving is not strongly related to college quality. Here the figures run from 38 to 25 percent.

	Emotional attachment to college	
College quality	*Strong*	*Not strong*
High	65	38
	(729)	(1,413)
Medium	55	35
	(607)	(1,750)
Low	37	25
	(719)	(2,493)

TABLE 73 *Percent who contributed to alma mater, by emotional attachment to college and college quality*

	Control			
	Private		Public	
	Emotional attachment		Emotional attachment	
College quality	Strong	Not strong	Strong	Not strong
High	73 (550)	42 (1,098)	40 (179)	33 (315)
Medium	59 (347)	52 (806)	50 (260)	20 (944)
Low	49 (281)	38 (938)	30 (438)	17 (1,555)

When the joint effects of all three independent variables are examined, the picture becomes quite confusing as far as college quality is concerned (Table 74). Among strongly attached alumni of private colleges, quality is strongly related to contributing; the percentages range from 73 in the best schools to 49 in the poorest. The relationship between quality and giving among alumni of public colleges who are not strongly attached is weaker, as the percentage range from 33 to 17 shows. In the other two combinations of attachment and control, the relation between quality and giving is mixed.

Private college graduates were consistently more likely to make a contribution to their college than were graduates of public colleges, usually by a wide margin. The same is true of the difference between those with strong and those with less strong emotional attachment.

One of the reasons that alumni of public colleges might be less likely to contribute may be that they come from less affluent families. As we have already seen, alumni whose parents were of higher SES were more likely than others to be donors. If it should turn out that the differences between graduates of public and private colleges disappeared when parental SES was controlled, the differences in generosity between graduates of the two types of institutions would merely stem from the kinds of students they were able to recruit.

In fact, parental SES operates very much like other variables that we have examined. As Table 75 shows, parental affluence had virtually no impact on public college alumni, whereas it was of considerable importance to graduates of private institutions. Among the latter the percentages range from 59 for the children of

	Control	
Parental SES	Private	Public
High	59 (1,494)	27 (856)
Medium high	50 (821)	25 (809)
Medium low	43 (695)	22 (876)
Low	37 (853)	21 (1,055)

TABLE 75
Percent who contributed to alma mater, by college control and parental socioeconomic status

the highest SES to 37 for the children of the lowest. The range was only 6 percentage points among public college alumni.

What about loyalty to alma mater? Does this variable give much hope for the public colleges? Table 76 adds emotional attachment to the items already included in Table 75. Turning first to the public colleges, we see that parental SES provides a little leverage among those who were strongly attached and virtually none among those with weaker attachment. In every comparison private college alumni were more likely to give than public college alumni. Similarly, persons with strong emotional attachment were consistently more likely to contribute.

Among public college graduates, the contribution rate fails to reach one-half even in the group most favorably disposed to alma mater, and it falls to one-sixth among those least favorably dis-

TABLE 76
Percent who contributed to alma mater, by college control, emotional attachment to college, and parental socioeconomic status

	Control			
	Private		Public	
	Emotional attachment		Emotional attachment	
Parental SES	Strong	Not strong	Strong	Not strong
High	75 (509)	52 (976)	42 (234)	21 (613)
Medium high	52 (241)	49 (569)	44 (170)	21 (616)
Medium low	51 (170)	40 (514)	36 (173)	19 (681)
Low	52 (205)	32 (642)	31 (266)	17 (777)

posed. On the other hand, three-quarters of the most favorably disposed private college alumni made contributions, compared to a third of those least favorably disposed.

SUMMARY AND CONCLUSIONS

This chapter has shown that alumni giving is related to three kinds of variables. The first is the characteristics of the school from which they graduated. Graduates of private colleges were more likely than graduates of public colleges to make a contribution to their alma mater. Among alumni of private colleges, those from the better colleges were more likely to be donors than were those from the poorer colleges. Graduates of independent liberal arts colleges were most likely to make contributions; those from state colleges were least likely to do so.

The second set of variables concerns one's loyalty or attachment to one's alma mater. Used in the analysis was a question asking about emotional attachment. Similar results would have been given using the desire to send one's oldest child to one's own college.

Finally, parental socioeconomic status was related to contributing. Alumni from the more affluent families were more likely to be donors than were those from less affluent ones. This was particularly true of private college graduates. Parental income predicts the making of a contribution more strongly than does the person's own current family income.

What conclusions can be drawn from these findings? We should, of course, remember that we are talking about one relatively recent college class. It is recent enough that a sizable fraction of the alumni are still getting started in careers and in family raising. These people may not be able to afford making much of a contribution. Against this possibility, however, we should balance the fact that income was only slightly related to giving. This could not have been the case if there had been many large gifts, but there were not.

Generally speaking, these findings look disturbingly like the results of many other survey research studies. On the face of it, the factors that help to predict whether a person will give money to his college tend not to be of the kind that the college might be able to change. Giving is related to characteristics of the institution, particularly whether it is public or private. Except for emotional attachment, nothing seems to increase greatly the probability that a public college alumnus will make a contribution. It seems a little unlikely that the multiversities are going to be able to do much to increase alumni loyalty in the present state of American higher education. There seems to be some evidence that winning football teams help raise the level of contributions. One need only point out that the production of such a phenomenon is transient, expensive, chancy, and potentially in conflict with other goals to realize that this is hardly the basis for a viable fiscal policy.

Facetious as this particular approach to raising money may seem to be, considerations such as the above raise an important issue. How much effort should be devoted to raising money from alumni? Their contributions seem to be quite small—though this finding may in part be a function of the recency of our alumni sample. Wouldn't intensive wooing of potentially large donors be much more effective? A cost-benefits analysis of intensive solicitation of alumni contributions might indicate that a high rate was useful in approaching the well-to-do, but tax laws favorable to large-scale giving would undoubtedly be more persuasive.

Part Two
Higher Education and Career Progress

8. The Transition from High School to College

Nearly everyone agrees that a college education is of considerable help in gaining entry to a middle-class occupation. There, however, the agreement ends. The basic fact that educational and occupational attainment are related is rarely disputed. The reasons why this relationship holds are a matter of considerable dispute.

For one thing, there is controversy regarding the extent to which a college education *should* provide career training. Many educators would give higher priority to other goals, such as the intellectual or personal development of their students. Since several goals of this kind have been covered in earlier chapters, we shall simply note their existence here and return to the issue of career preparation.

Does going to college prepare people for the jobs they will hold? If so, of what does this preparation consist? Does it train a person for the actual duties he will perform, or does it lend him a kind of general patina indicating that he will probably be acceptable in the upper-middle-class circles in which he may be expected to move? What kind of career preparation *can* a higher education give?

It obviously cannot replace on-the-job training. One need not adopt Paul Goodman's views on the desirability of wholesale apprenticeship in order to doubt that an undergraduate business curriculum will create managers of men or that education courses teach people how to teach. Moreover, even the kinds of careers heretofore thought conducive to direct vocational education are increasingly subject to rapid technological change. If, as seems likely, a person will need several doses of occupational retraining during his working life, the communication of rather specific information about the characteristics and duties of a job will be virtually useless.

If a college education does not provide direct occupational training, what does it do? One answer to this problem has been noted by a good many observers of higher education. As far as occupational preparation is concerned, a college degree indicates that a person has completed one stage in an elaborate process of finishing schooling. He may not know what to do in the actual job he enters, but his bachelor's degree certifies that he is acceptable material for a middle-class job (Jencks and Riesman, 1968, pp. 61–64).

Research that has tried to demonstrate the effects of college has had two kinds of results. Attempts to show that specific institutions have specific effects on their students have usually failed (Astin, 1968).[1] Assessments of the effects of going to college — any college — have come up with somewhat more positive results. Apparently the college experience produces people who are somewhat more independent, more tolerant, more open to new experiences, less rigid, and less prejudiced (Feldman and Newcomb, 1969). As far as we can tell, this kind of change is not much more likely to occur in one kind of an institution than in another, though a few well-known liberal arts colleges seem a little better at producing it. Presumably Harding College and Bob Jones University do not; they are not noted for doing so. On the whole, however, it seems to matter less what college one attends than that one attend college. One list of the rather bland virtues that are apparently produced by a college education runs as follows: "cosmopolitan, moderate, universalistic, somewhat legalistic, concerned with equity and fair play, aspiring to neutrality between regions, religions, and ethnic groups" (Jencks and Riesman, 1968, p. 12).

This could be a list of the qualities that a corporation might like to find in its executive trainees. At the same time, it is only a pallid reflection of the characteristics that are supposed to be produced by a "liberal" education. Perhaps the colleges have labored mightily to produce a swarm of gnats. In fact, the consistency with which a college education seems to produce students who are "nicer" as seniors than as freshmen is quite surprising in light of the diversity of aims professed by the institutions doing the job. The system is so large, so diversified, and so diffuse that to infer a means-end relation here would be nearly as fallacious as to do so with regard to statistical mechanics.

Though there is surely some sense in which a college education

[1] See also Astin (1962, 1963) and Holland (1957).

prepares a person to take his place in the labor force, a more pertinent question has to do with how higher education allocates its products to the economy. This is not a question of aims—whether educators are or are not trying to produce a highly trained elite labor force—but of functions. Given the fact that many employers demand a bachelor's degree for certain levels of jobs and that the professions usually require advanced degrees, higher education is the primary source of supply for elite occupational positions.

In fact, the entire American educational system operates as a device for screening people according to their intellectual abilities and academic performance. Even before a child is first placed in an educational track, he is measured and assessed in ways that will help to determine his ultimate occupational fate. The various diplomas and degrees serve as gateways to successively higher occupational levels. In gross terms, a high school diploma provides reasonable entry to upper-blue-collar and lower-white-collar jobs; a bachelor's degree provides entry to many middle- and upper-white-collar jobs, especially in business and schoolteaching; and advanced degrees provide access to certain elite professions (Davis, 1963).

There is no doubt that a college degree is a very real advantage for membership in the middle class. Drawing on 1950 census data, Davis (1963) found that for all age groups, college graduation was a virtual necessity for being in a professional occupation. Among the oldest male workers, a high school diploma made the odds favoring a white-collar occupation 3:2. Among the youngest, the odds were almost exactly reversed. Among all age groups, only about 10 percent of the college graduates were in blue-collar jobs. Chances of a high school graduate being in a profession have always been slight. And the men who had entered but not completed college were slowly being pushed out of the middle class. In short, graduation from college is becoming increasingly important for entry into middle-class occupations, though it has long been necessary for entry into the professions.

In fact, it is clear that the most important single pre-occupational experience determining a person's occupational achievements is educational attainment, with the amount of schooling partially dependent on parental characteristics and partially dependent on IQ (Blau and Duncan, 1967; Duncan, 1968; Duncan, Featherman, and Duncan, 1968). Father's educational and occupational attainment make substantial and roughly equal contributions toward explaining respondents' educational attainment. IQ is about twice as strong as either of the other two variables. Furthermore, intelligence adds substantially to the explanation of respondents' education vis-à-vis both socioeconomic variables. IQ independently accounts for 16 percent of the variance in educational attainment. The entire set of independent variables (including number of siblings) accounts for 42 percent, leaving 58 percent still unexplained (Duncan et al., 1968, pp. 80–119). A major reduction in the unexplained variance could come about only by the introduction of a variable that was highly related to the dependent variable, but not to the independent variables already taken into account. In other words, variables at all closely related to parental SES or ability will add little to the level of explanation, though they might specify the processes involved in greater detail.

In any case, chances for improving the prediction of educational attainment do not seem great. Pessimism regarding such predictions is justified on grounds other than possible theoretical inadequacies. Part of the variation in educational attainment undoubtedly stems from the operation of chance. Part is also due to measurement error. We can think of some part of the chance factor as a matter of accidents in the life histories of particular people. Some will become ill, others suffer accidents, others get a good break. It is impossible to assess the importance of such matters, at least on an aggregate level, because the measurement of chance must be done negatively—as the unexplained variance remaining after more systematic variables are taken into account. Only if we had a perfect theory of educational attainment would this procedure be acceptable. Since such a theory is unattainable in principle, let alone in practice, we can only speculate on the role of chance in the processes to be discussed in this chapter.

Clearly, education is a very important path to the achievement of occupational status. The Blau-Duncan (1967) analysis allows us not only to assess the importance of education but to explain, at least in part, how it operates. Let us turn to the impact of father's education, father's occupation, and son's education on the son's first job. In the first place, a man's own educational attainment is a more important determinant of his first-job prestige than are the socioeconomic characteristics of his father. Nonetheless, his father's prestige has an important direct effect, as well as an indirect one through the advantage given by education. The effect of father's education takes place entirely through its influence on son's education.

When IQ is included in the picture, it neither adds much to the explained variance, which is about one-third of the total, nor detracts much from the direct contribution of father's occupation. One of the reasons that education seemed to be so important, however, is that being smart helps a person get more education and also contributes directly to the prestige of his first job.

Finally, an analysis of a synthetic cohort — no one has followed the careers of a representative age group through the life cycle, so different age groups were compared — shows that both father's occupation and respondent's education are decreasingly important as a career matures. Prior occupations become increasingly important; and the older one is, the more closely related a prior occupation is to a subsequent one (Blau and Duncan, 1967, Ch. 5; Duncan et al., 1968, pp. 80–119).

Though our primary concern will be with the influence of progress through the system of higher education, we shall also assess the effects of the transition from high school to college with data on 1960 high school senior males provided by Project Talent. These data allow us to address two important questions: Who goes to college, and what effects does college entrance have on a young person's occupational plans? The analysis of these problems will be the subject of this chapter. Chapter 9 will then examine the role of higher education in occupational attainment. Before the actual analysis can begin, however, we must deal with two prior matters: the definition and measurement of occupational attainment, and the statistical methods to be used in this chapter and the next.

OCCUPA-TIONAL PRESTIGE　The observation that higher education is increasingly important in the allocation of persons to and within the labor force is certainly not original with us. Many observers of the "knowledge society" have made this point in connection with the idea that knowledge producers and knowledge transmitters play a major role in the modern economy (Bell, 1966, 1967; Galbraith, 1967; Jencks and Riesman, 1968, esp. pp. 8–20; Kahn and Wiener, 1967; Servan-Schreiber, 1968). Their argument usually seems to imply that all knowledge workers are important and rarely attempts to discuss which kinds might be most important.

The general public are not so bashful. Though no one has ever asked them to rate occupations according to their potential for contributing to the knowledge society, other questions have gotten at much the same kind of thing. If people are asked to rate the "general standing" of an occupation, they will do so with striking consistency. Ratings taken at widely separated time intervals are consistent with each other; such ratings are consistent across national boundaries; they are consistent between random and haphazard samples and between questions asking for actual ratings and questions asking for rankings (Blau and Duncan, 1967; Counts, 1925; Hodge, Siegel, and Rossi, 1966; Hodge, Treiman, and Rossi, 1966; Inkeles and Rossi, 1956; National Opinion Research Center, 1953; Smith, 1943). The criterion of general standing is consistent with others more directly relevant to education and knowledge, such as the amount of skill necessary or the amount of training required.

The great consistency of occupational ratings across time and place and the consensus among broad groups of the population indicate that occupational prestige is a stable dimension of social reality. But what does it have to do with more objective aspects of the social order? The answer is a great deal. Using the 1950 percentage of people in an occupation who had incomes of $3,500 or more and the percentage who had graduated from high school or better, Duncan (1961) was able to predict the occupation's prestige with great accuracy. In other words, the prestige of an occupation is closely related to the level of education and income attained by its members. The respect which people are granted in connection with their occupation is reflected in two basic pieces of factual information about that occupation.

Recently a National Opinion Research Center (NORC) survey has, by direct questioning, arrived at scores for over 200 census occupation categories (Hodge and Siegel, 1964). These scores will be used in this analysis.

As we have already indicated, our concern in this chapter will be with variables that influence college attendance and occupational plans. In particular, three sets of variables will be discussed here, the first pertaining to a person's intellectual ability and academic performance, the second dealing with his parents' socioeconomic status (SES), and the third dealing with his own desires and plans held when he was a senior in high school.

In the first group are the following variables: the person's intellectual ability measured by a scale whose items are similar in content to a college entrance test; the kind of track or curriculum to which the person was assigned in high school—college preparatory versus all other kinds; and his high school grades. The second set includes only one variable, a composite measure of the socioeconomic status of the parental home. Items used in this index include parental family income, father's occupation, the educational level attained by both parents, and the presence or absence of certain amenities in the home, such as a room of one's own or books and magazines.

The third set includes the person's occupational plans given at two points in time — the senior year in high school and one year later.[2] The latter is the ultimate dependent variable in the analysis to be reported in this chapter. Means, standard deviations, and frequencies for variables are presented in Table 77. Though it will not be explicitly used in the causal model to be dealt with here, the occupation the person desired as a high school senior will be discussed. In the next chapter, similar data on college alumni will be among early variables in a model assessing the impact of higher education on career allocation.

Since the occupational world is far more important to men than to women and since the analysis of the next chapter is limited to men, the results reported in this chapter apply to men only.

[2] Parental SES is a combination of father's education, mother's education, father's occupation, family income, the value of the parental home, the presence of books and appliances in the home, the presence of TV and radio, and whether the respondent had a room of his own. The measure of intellectual ability is "Information, Part I," which resembles in content a college entrance examination. High school curriculum refers to answers to a question on the kind of high school program that a person was in; the score was 1 if the answer was "college preparatory" and 0 otherwise. High school prestige scores were measured by assigning prestige scores based on a recent NORC survey to the thirty-five categories of two closed questions on occupational plans, one referring to "the occupation you *expect* to make your career after you have completed your education," and the other to the occupation "you would most *like* to enter." College plans were scored as follows: males who said that they definitely planned to attend college full time were scored 5; those who said they definitely did not plan to attend college were scored 1; those choosing one of the three middle categories were assigned appropriate intermediate scores. College attendance or entrance refers to having attended a college, university, or junior college for at least part of the 1960–61 academic year; it is scored 1 versus 0. Post–high school prestige expectations are NORC scores assigned to a four-digit occupation code based on responses to an open question asked in the Project Talent one-year follow-up. This classification differs most markedly from that of the census by its greater emphasis on occupational activities rather than job titles. One of the writers converted these categories into census job titles and thence to NORC scores. For the most part, such conversions were quite straightforward. Further discussion of the questions and scales may be found in Flanagan et al. (1964, pp. B−1–10, K−1–23) and Flanagan and Cooley (1966, pp. E−10–11, A−2–8). The data have been weighted to allow for the original sample design and to account for bias stemming from failure to respond to the follow-up questionnaire.

Variable	Mean	Standard deviation	Unweighted N
Parental SES	98.76	10.60	4,794
Intellectual ability	152.80	37.00	4,923
High school curriculum	.47	.50	4,736
High school grades	2.32	.99	4,609
High school prestige expected	58.65	12.64	3,873
High school prestige desired	59.37	12.54	3,987
College plans	3.18	1.57	4,392
College attendance	.44	.50	5,015
Post–high school prestige expectation	54.79	14.26	3,318

Simply by establishing a temporal ordering among the variables just named, we can outline a theory that partially accounts for the occupational plans of young men in the process of making the transition from high school to college.

Starting at the beginning, we have two variables—parental SES and the individual's own intellectual ability. The first can be viewed as the amount of head start provided by growing up in a relatively affluent and well-informed family. The second, of course, represents the person's own intellectual qualifications, which will ultimately be important not only for his educational but for his occupational achievements. Even though parental characteristics can be viewed as prior to those of a child, no attempt will be made to establish a causal ordering here. To do so in a meaningful way would require a solution of the heredity-environment problem because one of the determinants of a person's IQ is the IQ of his parents. The temptation to commit infinite regress is quickly dispelled by the difficulty of collecting relevant data.

The next variable in the sequence is the kind of curriculum that the person was in when he was attending high school. The implications of this variable for college attendance are obvious. Assessment of its role in this regard will also involve noting the extent to which assignment to a college preparatory track is related to parental SES and intellectual ability.

After curriculum comes the grades earned by the person when he was in high school. Both this variable and its predecessor are clearly relevant to college admissions and therefore to college entrance. If going to college has an effect on one's career plans, both grades and curriculum will also play a role in the explanation of career plans.

The next step in the process refers to the person's own plans or desires. During his senior year in high school, each respondent was asked to select from a list both the occupation he would expect to make his career after he completed his education and the one he would "most like to enter." Each of these was assigned an NORC occupational prestige score. Partly because expectations are used in Chapter 9 and partly because they are a little more closely related to later career outcomes, occupational expectations have been emphasized in this analysis.

Since planning to attend college is known to be a strong predictor of actual college attendance, college plans have been included here. The actual question referred to the definiteness of one's plans for attending a college or junior college full time "after you leave high school."

In a causal model of the kind being developed here, it is very important that all but the initial variables be treated as if they were clearly ordered in time. The two variables just mentioned present some problems in this regard. One could plausibly argue that career plans determine college plans on the grounds that a person goes to college to further his occupational plans. It is also possible, however, to argue that college plans determine one's occupational goals; if a person expects to go to college he will also expect to be in an occupation appropriate to his eventual educational attainment. We have chosen to adopt the first approach here on the grounds that it seems somewhat more plausible than the second.

There is no question of the temporal ordering of the set of variables dealing with high school and before in relation to the set pertaining to the year after high school. The first group of questions was asked in the last year of high school, and the second was asked one year later.

Even though the question on college attendance was asked at the same time as the one on career expectations, we can still infer that the former is prior to the latter. By the beginning of the last term in an academic year, a person loses the opportunity to go to college in that year if he is not already there. His status with regard to college attendance has become fixed. The possibility of a change in career plans remains open. For our purposes a person is treated as having attended (entered) a college whether he was studying full or part time and whether he reported that he had dropped out or not.

It is worth emphasizing that the findings to be reported will constitute a description of the *process* by which a young man makes his occupational plans. In the model proposed here we treat that process as having several stages, starting with two variables, intellectual ability and parental SES. The next step is allocation to a high school track, the next is academic performance in high school, then high school career plans, planning for college, going to college, and, finally, career plans held in the year following high school graduation. Each step in this process is treated as dependent on all prior stages.

Fortunately, there is a statistical method that allows us to proceed in the manner outlined above. Unfortunately, the method is rather technical and calls for a fairly extensive background in statistics for full understanding. Knowing that many readers do not have such a background, we shall try to give a general, nontechnical explanation of the method.

PATH ANALYSIS The technique to be employed here, *path analysis,* was developed by Sewall Wright, who used it in research in genetics. Its utility for sociology has been best described by Duncan (1966). Here we shall simply try to give a general idea of the method's uses, assumptions, and limitations.

Path analysis is a method for presenting a causal model in which a series of independent variables is used to predict a series of dependent variables. In this chapter, the background characteristics (parental SES and intellectual ability) will be used to explain allocation to a high school track. Then all three variables, plus those that come after curriculum but before senior expectations, such as grades, will be used to predict high school senior expectations. The latter will then be included in the set of predictors of college plans, which will become a predictor of college attendance, which in turn will be used to account for post–high school prestige expectations.

A set of computations needs to be done for each step of the model, but the entire model can be shown in one diagram. As the above indicates, the dependent variable—the one being predicted— changes with each phase of the process. The actual computations involve solving several sets of simultaneous equations formed by all or some of the correlations of the independent variables with each other and the correlations of each independent variable with the dependent variable.[3] The results of these computations yield a numerical estimate of the direct effect of each independent variable on the dependent variable. The method of computation means that each estimate of a direct effect, or path, is given with the effects of the other independent variables controlled.

There are, then, two kinds of paths, *direct* and *indirect*. The former are given by the calculations mentioned above and are a measure of the direct influence of one variable on another, *within a given causal scheme*. Addition of variables to or omission of variables from a causal system can change the values of a direct path coefficient dramatically. Indirect paths will vary in complexity. In a causal model with many independent variables, indirect paths may show intricate relationships, starting at the beginning of a model and making their way through intervening variables to the dependent variable. The value for all indirect paths involving an independent variable is the difference between the simple (zero-order) correlation of that independent variable with the dependent variable and the direct path linking the two. The percentage of a variable's effects that are direct is thus given by dividing the direct path by the zero-order correlation.

Another distinction between kinds of effects needs to be mentioned. The total effects of a variable are given by its zero-order correlation with the dependent variable. This correlation is inflated by redundancy between independent variables, two of which may, for example, partially measure the same thing. The effects given by the direct path remove such redundancy. One may also distinguish between *genuine* and *spurious* effects, which are defined in terms of one's causal model. Genuine effects include all direct effects plus the indirect effects of a variable not attributable to earlier variables operating as causes of it. Indirect effects brought about by the operation of such common causes spuriously inflate the impact of a variable. These need to be eliminated. Indirect effects showing how the influence of one variable is transmitted to another through one or more intervening variables must not be confused with spurious effects and should not be partialed out when assessing the importance of an independent variable.

An example may help to clarify how a path analysis would work.

[3] The technically oriented reader will realize that this is a description of multiple regression analysis. The path coefficients are standardized net regression weights.

A simple three-variable model will serve to convey the basic ideas. Consider the assertion that *A* causes *B*, which in turn causes *C*. One way of representing this statement would be with the following diagram:

A———→B———→C

This means not only that *A* causes *B* and *B* causes *C* but that all *A*'s effects on *C* are transmitted through *B*. An alternative model would be:

This diagram means that *A* causes *B* and *B* causes *C*, that part of *A*'s effects on *C* are transmitted through *B*, but that part are direct. One would choose between the two models by examining the direct path from *A* to *C*. If its value is nil, then the first model would describe the causal system involving these three variables. If its value is not negligible, the second model would be appropriate. Introduction of other variables between *A* and *B* or *B* and *C* could change the interpretation, however, and might lead to an interpretation analogous to that of the first model.

To conclude this discussion, we should draw attention to some of the assumptions and limitations of path analysis. The first of these is that the method demands a "complete" causal explanation of every dependent variable. Given the well-known inability of sociological theory to explain all of anything, it might seem necessary to abandon the method. The demand is only a formal one, however. Expressing the amount of variation of any given variable in percentage terms means, of course, that there is a variation of 100 percent to be explained by a set of independent variables. The joint effect of all variables actually used in the model is expressed by the coefficient of multiple correlation, *R*. R^2 states the proportion of variance in the dependent variable explained by its correlation with a given set of independent variables. It follows that $(1 - R^2)$ is the proportion of variance unexplained by a given model. The square root of this quantity, or $\sqrt{(1 - R^2)}$, gives the value of the final path coefficient in a complete model. Since this path is a measure of the effects of everything left out of a given causal model, it is called a *residual path*. It can be viewed as the sum of all paths from unmeasured variables not included in the model to the dependent variable. Residual variables could include measurement error or variables that a better theory would have taken into account. To contribute much to the explanatory power of a model, however, the new variables must be largely independent of other independent variables in the model and highly related to the dependent variable—otherwise they will not add much that is new. Addition of such variables could alter the workings of the model by showing how the effect of one variable was transmitted through another or by showing that the effects of one variable were really caused by another, but the new variables would not markedly increase the proportion of variance explained.

Variables must be measured quantitatively, and each should be distributed in a fashion at least approximating the normal curve. Furthermore, since linear measures of correlation are used, the relations among variables are assumed to be linear. A plot of the joint distribution of two variables should be rather well approximated by a straight line. If a curve fits markedly better, linear correlation coefficients will be inaccurate and the model distorted. In addition, no variables are taken as causes of themselves, a seemingly trivial requirement that actually rules out such things as feedback mechanisms. This problem is not particularly great. In this analysis, for example, prestige expectations held during high school are taken as causes of expectations held one year later. This is perfectly legitimate since the variables were measured at the two different times.

COLLEGE ATTENDANCE AND OCCUPATIONAL CAREER PLANS As we have already mentioned, the first step in the process culminating in career plans held a year after high school is allocation to a college preparatory or other program in high school. Only two determinants are available at this stage of the model, parental SES and the person's own intellectual ability. These two variables are of considerable conceptual and practical importance, because despite the purportedly "meritocratic" criterion by which such allocation is supposed to be carried out, it is widely known that parental privilege plays a role.

One estimate of the importance of parental SES is given in Figure 1, which contains direct path coefficients for the entire model. (Table 78 presents the zero-order correlations on which this figure is based.) The coefficient linking parental SES and curriculum is .26, indicating that the former independently accounts for about 7 percent of the variance in the latter. Ability is a strong variable,

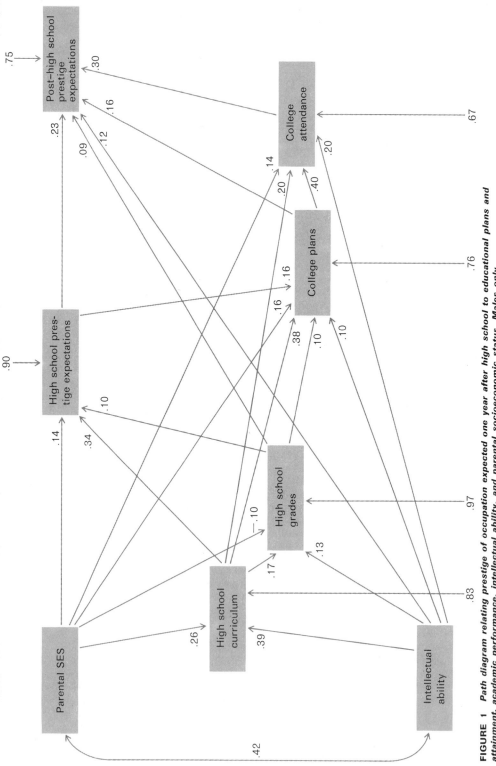

FIGURE 1 *Path diagram relating prestige of occupation expected one year after high school to educational plans and attainment, academic performance, intellectual ability, and parental socioeconomic status. Males only.*

TABLE 78 *Correlations between variables used in analysis of college attendance and post–high school prestige expectations (Pearson r)*

Variable	Intellectual ability	High school curriculum	High school grades	High school prestige expected	High school prestige desired	College plans	College attendance	Post–high school prestige expectations
Parental SES	.42	.43	.03	.29	.25	.41	.47	.36
Intellectual ability		.50	.18	.29	.30	.42	.53	.43
High school curriculum			.20	.42	.34	.58	.59	.44
High school grades				.17	.20	.23	.21	.25
High school prestige expected			·		.81	.41	.37	.46
High school prestige desired						.38	.34	.43
College plans							.65	.52
College attendance								.58

with a direct path of .39, which independently accounts for about 15 percent of the variance in curriculum. Together, the two variables account for 31 percent of the variance in assignment to tracks; thus, 9 percent (31—15—7) must be attributed to the joint operation of the two variables. With the present model, it is not possible to allocate further this 9 percent.

We should note the value of the residual path (.83) at the head of the first arrow originating at the bottom of the page. A path coefficient this large, in addition to the ones explicitly in the diagram, is required to explain 100 percent of the variance in assignment to curricula. This residual effect is in the same metric as that for other path coefficients. In order to convert it to a percentage of the variance, it is necessary to square it, which yields a value of .69. This is the percentage of the variance *not* explained by the two variables in the model.

Here, as elsewhere, we run into problems of evaluating the size of the coefficients involved. Several questions need to be discussed under this heading. First, are there any relative standards to indicate how "good" an explanation these two variables provide? We know that we have fallen short of perfection by 69 percent, but a glance at the values of the residual paths running across the top and bottom of this figure shows that we will never come close to meeting the absolute standard of perfection. Could we expect that better measures of the two variables might explain more of the variance? The answer to this question is almost certainly in the affirmative, but we cannot tell how much improvement in measurement might improve prediction because we do not know how unreliable our measures are. Viewed as a measure of IQ, the index used here is doubtless not as good as a more traditional one. The items in the SES index include ones traditionally deemed to measure this concept; nonetheless, the pertinent questions could doubtless have been more reliably asked and answered. On the other hand, it is almost certain that omission of one or another item from the SES index would alter the correlations of SES with other variables hardly at all.

These considerations indicate that better measures of the two independent variables would reduce the unexplained variance in allocation to a high school curriculum. With the data available to us, however, we cannot say how much better an explanation more reliable measures might produce. We can, however, be sure that the two variables would still fall far short of explaining *all* the variance.

One can also ask what other variables might be important in this process. It is not hard to think of one that is undoubtedly of great importance — race. There seems little doubt that, even at the same levels of SES and intelligence, fewer black than white students will be placed in college preparatory programs. This fact is undoubtedly true today; it was probably truer in 1960, when the pertinent data were collected. For one thing, Negroes are more likely than whites to attend schools that have no tracking system. For another, they are probably discouraged from attempting to get into academic tracks, and for another, they are doubtless discriminated against in this regard as in so many others. Unfortunately, Project Talent did not collect data on race, so we cannot tell exactly how influential this factor might be.

The second set of issues having to do with findings such as these deals with their bearing on questions of social policy. How much impact *should* parental affluence have on the allocation of a person to a college preparatory program? If the answer is none, the relevant path coefficient should be zero. Is the difference between this path coefficient of zero and the value actually found a measure of social injustice? If so, how is this particular aspect of injustice brought about — through the middle-class or racial bias of counselors and teachers or through the provision of tracking in some parts of the country and not in others? A further question, to which we shall return later, is the way in which allocation to an academic track serves to transmit the influence of parental SES to college attendance and career plans.

An even more knotty issue than that involved with SES effects is the "proper" size of the relation between intelligence and allocation to a track. Whatever the problems connected with the present measure of ability, we can be sure that all such measures are far from perfect. Decisions based on them can never be entirely reliable. The extent to which they are biased against members of minority groups is another argument against complete reliance on such tests. These considerations are rather familiar ones, even though controversy about the reliability of tests as sorting devices still continues.

A perfect test, if one could be devised, only raises the question of whether facility in dealing with abstract symbols, the talent measured by most IQ tests, would be appropriate as the sole criterion of allocation to college preparatory curricula and thus to college and beyond. The fact that talents other than the academic are important in later life leads to a negative answer. Michael Young's (1959) speculations about the kind of society one might expect under narrowly academic meritocratic standards are also to the point. Intellectual "merit" will produce a stratification system as easily as any other criterion. A society like Young's twenty-first-century England, in which the results of mental tests seal one's occupational fate, is at least as rigid as the one we have now.

The fact is that there is no agreement on how important family background or intelligence should be in the process of allocation to different slots in the occupational world. Perhaps a majority of the populace would agree that parental privilege is currently too important and intelligence not strong enough. This is the only basis for deciding that the values shown here are inappropriate. Neither the numbers we have computed nor the theory that relates them to other such numbers can answer questions such as this.

We shall not dwell long on the explanation of high school grades. The effects of this variable are too small to be of much importance but too large to be ignored. The low zero-order correlation between grades and ability (.18) makes us suspect that the question used to ask about grades was inadequate. If so, the estimates of its effects are underestimated. The low value of the path from ability (.13) is produced by the low zero-order correlation. The —.10 path from SES is rather interesting. Apparently sons of affluent families do not work quite as hard as others and therefore get somewhat poorer grades. The low zero-order correlation between ability and grades is part of the reason that curriculum seems so important, with a path of .17. Allowance is clearly made for the different abilities of persons in different tracks, or there would be no correlation between grades and curriculum.

Figure 1 indicates that the prestige associated with the career occupation expected by a young man as a high school senior is a direct function of three variables: parental SES, high school curriculum, and high school grades, with curriculum being the strongest of the three. The coefficient of .34 is independent of each of the three earlier variables in the model. No matter how it is that a person finds himself in a college preparatory program, the fact that he is in one will cause him to raise his occupational sights, and the fact that he is not in one will cause him to lower his sights. Even though ability's effects are indirect, as the absence of an arrow indicates, they are not negligible. Only that part of the simple correlation of .29 associated with SES reduces this correlation as a measure of the effects of this variable. The largest of the indirect paths from ability passes through curriculum. The value of an indirect path is given by the product of the paths making it up; in this case $(.39)(.34) = .13$. This is nearly half of the simple correlation.

The most important message of this segment of the analysis involves the role of high school tracks. It seems likely that assignment to a track in the early years of high school will have rather far-reaching consequences.

As mentioned earlier, college plans have been included primarily because they are a potent predictor of college attendance. Before looking at the effects of this variable, we shall examine some of its determinants. The most powerful of these is allocation to a high school track. The direct path from this variable to college plans is .38. All other paths are much smaller, though none is negligible. The .16 from family SES is just as large as the .16 from senior expectations. The ability and grades paths are also of an equal size, .10. Again, we must note zero-order correlations. That between SES and college plans is .41; that between ability and plans is .42. Major indirect paths from both variables pass through high school curriculum, .10 from SES and .15 from ability. Allocation to a college preparatory curriculum is important not only in its own right but in transmitting the effects of ability and family background.

The residual of .76 indicates that 58 percent of the variance in college plans is unexplained, 42 percent explained. With problems of this kind, accounting for this proportion of the variance is a respectable achievement. The nontrivial direct paths from the two earliest variables are of greater concern than the rather large amount of variance unexplained. From the substantive point of view, these nontrivial direct paths indicate that a theory involving the variables in this model is not able to gain from the parsimony of dropping earlier variables in the explanation of later ones. To the extent that the direct paths from SES and ability are not zero, we do not know how their effects are transmitted. Presumably something is missing from the model.

College attendance is one of the two chief dependent variables in this analysis. It refers to attendance at a college or a junior college during some part of the academic year following high school graduation. Note that planning on going to college is by far the strongest predictor of actually doing so. Independent of all six earlier variables in the model, the path from plans to actuality is .40. High school curriculum has a direct path of .20 and an indirect path linking curriculum to college plans and college attendance of .15. Intellectual ability has a direct path of .20; its largest indirect path, .08, runs through curriculum to college attendance. The direct effect of parental SES is given by the path of .14. The largest interpretable indirect path runs through college plans with a value of .06. The next largest runs through curriculum with a value of .05.

So far, we have discussed the value of direct paths and prominent indirect ones. Interpretation of the direct paths must rely on the fact that the value of one is independent of the effects of all other variables in the model. One conclusion to be drawn from the rather sizable direct paths involving SES, ability, and curriculum is that these effects are not entirely transmitted by the influence they have on college plans. Another way of saying the same thing is to note that the earlier variables have an influence on the *realization* of college plans.

The direct paths from earlier variables give a misleading picture of the independent effects of these variables, however. Table 79 gives the values for the independent contributions of each of the variables in this model. Parental SES and ability are treated as initial conditions, and the first column of the table shows the contribution of each, independent of the other. Here we see that ability is the stronger of the two variables, with a path of .40 in contrast to the .30 for SES, a contribution which is by no means negligible.

TABLE 79 *Determinants of college attendance (Standardized net regression weights)*

Variable	Parental SES and intellectual ability	High school curriculum	High school grades	High school prestige expectations	College plans
Parental SES	.30	.20	.21	.20	.14
Intellectual ability	.40	.25	.24	.23	.20
High school curriculum		.38	.36	.33	.19
High school grades			.09	.08	.04
High school prestige expectations				.09	.03
College plans					.38
R^2	.35	.45	.46	.46	.55
R	.59	.67	.68	.68	.74

Even though we cannot solve the heredity-environment problem here, it is worth noting that the contribution of parental intelligence to a child's intelligence that is transmitted by SES would be a part of the indirect not the direct path. Therefore the .30 cannot be attributed to this cause. Here we see one of the ways in which social privilege is handed down from one generation to the next. The next to bottom row (R^2) indicates that the two variables together explain 35 percent of the variance in college attendance.

Allocation to a high school curriculum has a marked influence of its own, as its direct path of .38 in the second column of the table indicates. (The procedure for assessing independent influences is to regress college attendance on a given independent variable and control for its "causes" but not its "effects.") The comparison between the first and second column shows that curriculum is an important transmitter of the effects of the earlier variables. We can infer this fact from the drop in the coefficient for ability from .40 to .25 when curriculum is introduced into the system. Similarly the path from SES drops from .30 to .20. High school curriculum explains an additional 10 percent of the variance; R^2 increases from .35 to .45. By the standards of most sociological analysis, we have already done a respectable job of explaining college attendance.

By any standards, the next two variables—high school grades and prestige expectations—are not important in explaining college attendance. Their direct paths are small, .09, so they independently explain very little of the variance. They are also rather weak transmitters of the influence of earlier variables. Here again we see grounds for being suspicious of the way in which grades are measured. Not only are they weakly related to ability, they are weakly related to college attendance. Since we can be reasonably sure that the true state of affairs is otherwise, we must remember that a more adequately measured variable would (1) explain more of the variance and (2) account for more of the indirect effects of earlier variables.

College plans, on the other hand, are potent predictors of college attendance. Since this finding is tantamount to discovering that people tend to do what they say they expect to do, it should be no occasion for surprise. It does obliquely raise an important issue, however. What if we could have taken a person's desires for a college education into account? To what extent would motivation have produced a different result? Though we do not have data that assess this question with regard to college attendance, we do have such data pertaining to senior occupational desires as contrasted with expectations. These will be discussed in detail later. Suffice it to say that if educational desires are related to educational expectations in the way that occupational desires are related to occupational expectations, the desires would do very little to flesh out our story. If so, expectations and desires can be treated interchangeably, and at least part of the contribution of expectations can be seen as being produced by a form of motivation operating independently of ability, family background, and the functioning of the educational system.

What role does going to college play in the occupational plans of a young man? As Figure 1 shows, college attendance is the most important direct determinant of a person's occupational plans. In fact, college attendance even overshadows occupational plans held a year earlier. The ordering of the nonnegligible direct paths determining post–high school prestige expectations runs college attendance, high school expectations, college plans, intellectual ability, and high school grades.

The crucial point is that success or failure in attending college does indeed change a young man's career plans. If he goes to college, he is likely to raise his expectations; if he does not, he is likely to lower them. On the other hand, the experience of going to college does not have an overwhelming influence on career plans. Senior plans continue to be a substantial influence, with a path coefficient of .23, as do college plans, with a coefficient of .16.

Perhaps the continued effectiveness of these variables, net of college attendance, can tell us something about the process of change in career plans. For one thing, the question on college plans did not refer to "next year." The fact that a person planning to attend college did not do so in the year immediately following high school does not necessarily mean that he will never attend college. The expectation of ultimately attending college may be enough to prevent a change in career plans regardless of the immediate reality.

The reader will note that little attention has been paid to the path of .09 leading from grades and the path of .12 leading from ability. The effects of the latter may stem partly from the content of the test used in this analysis. As we have already noted, the measure is quite similar in content to a college entrance examination. Since colleges use such examinations as criteria for admission, it may be that a purer indicator of ability would not have such large direct effects. If not, the failure to account for more of ability's effects is a flaw of the model. A more adequate scheme could be expected to make ability's direct effects more nearly zero.

The omission in the diagram of direct paths from parental SES and high school curriculum indicates that the direct contributions of these two variables are negligible.

With the exception of the coefficient originating with college attendance, the data in Figure 1 do not tell us "really" how important any of the earlier variables are. Table 80, which is based on the same principle as Table 79, contains this information.

An overview of the independent contributions of each of the variables can be gained by looking at the two entries in the first column and the bottom entries in each of the others. The strongest variable is ability, with a coefficient of .34; the weakest is grades, .16. Next come college attendance, .29; high school expectations, .28; college plans, .27; and high school curriculum, .25. Parental SES is the second weakest variable, with an independent contribution of .22. The entire set of variables explains 44 percent of the variance, an amount equal to that explained by the more limited set shown in Figure 1.

Reading along the rows of the table shows that high school curriculum is important in transmitting the effects of both prior variables.

TABLE 80 *Determinants of post–high school prestige expectations (Standardized net regression weights)*

Variable	Parental SES and intellectual ability	High school curriculum	High school grades	High school prestige expectations	College plans	College attendance
Parental SES	.22	.16	.17	.14	.10	.05
Intellectual ability	.34	.24	.22	.20	.17	.12
High school curriculum		.25	.22	.14	.03	—.02
High school grades			.16	.13	.10	.09
High school prestige expectations				.28	.23	.22
College plans					.27	.16
College attendance						.29
R^2	.23	.27	.30	.36	.40	.44

The effects of curriculum are mostly transmitted by senior expectations and college plans. It is hardly surprising that a sizable part of the effects of college plans are transmitted through actual college attendance.

SUMMARY Such are the details of the analysis. The general picture they make is an important one. Clearly, a young man's progress through the educational system is an important influence on his career plans. Allocation to a high school track is apparently a significant form of feedback from the system, one that influences a person's college and career plans. Though the effects of grades are weaker, they can be viewed in the same way. The procedures by which the system screens and sorts the people it processes have a significant impact on their plans and behavior.

Nevertheless, the model discussed here falls far short of a complete explanation. Despite the fact that explaining 44 percent of the variance is respectable enough by sociological standards, one is entitled to wonder what other variables might affect a person's occupational plans. An obvious candidate is some measure of motivation. Presumably, a young man who particularly wants to be in a desirable occupation will try hard to gain such a position. If so, one could expect success-oriented motivation to have an independent effect on occupational expectations and to contribute to the amount of variance explained.

As was noted when this model was introduced, a question was asked on the occupational desires of the person when he was a high school senior. Though this is surely the most pertinent measure of motivation that we could have found, it suffers from resting on no foundation of psychological theory. A more psychologically oriented measure of ambition would have been a better choice from this point of view. That such a measure has little impact on actual occupational attainment leads us to suspect that its impact on expectations would be equally slight (Duncan et al., 1968, pp. 131–181). The more direct measure is potentially more powerful. It also happens to be the only one available.

No detailed discussion of results is necessary here because the occupation desired behaves in almost exactly the same way as the occupation expected. Path coefficients from the former are slightly smaller than those from the latter. Added to a model already containing expectations, the desires contribute nothing to the proportion of variance explained. In models containing both variables, the two essentially "split the difference." Path coefficients from one are nearly equal to those from the other. The zero-order correlation of .81 between the two variables explains why. The two variables measure essentially the same thing.

The above does not mean that motivation is unimportant, though it does indicate that a "purified" motivation effect cannot be separated from the effects of plans and expectations. The findings just reported indicate that desires and expectations can be treated as one variable. Separating out the motivational component of this variable is not possible, at least with these data.

This chapter has served two purposes. It has documented the rather well-known fact that college attendance has a considerable impact on a person's occupational choices. At the same time it has shown in greater detail how a person's experiences in the educational system alter his career decisions. By doing this, we have set the stage for the next chapter, which will show how a man's progress through the higher educational system affects not only his career decisions but his actual occupational attainment. We shall start where we ended here — with the freshman year in college.

9. Higher Education and Occupational Attainment

With Chapter 8 as background, we may move rather directly to the concerns of this one. The method of analysis will be the same, and the variables used will be similar. The basic question to be dealt with here is: How is a man's occupational attainment, seven years out of college, conditioned by his experiences with the higher educational system during and after college? One of the variables likely to influence the kind of job a person holds is the kind of job he expects to hold. Data on the job held are available for 1968. Data on expectations are available for the freshman year in college from questions administered in 1961. The 1961 questionnaire also contains the person's career choice made when he was a senior. In 1964, career expectations held three years after graduation were ascertained.

One aspect of this analysis will thus deal with the relation between plans and reality. How well, four years in advance, can men "predict" in what occupation they will be engaged? Another phase is related to the consistency of the expectations themselves. How changeable are career plans over the period from the freshman year in college to three years after graduation?

It is reasonable to assume that this particular group of men — college graduates headed for relatively prestigious careers — will be rather consistent in their occupational plans and that the relation between plans and actual occupation will be quite high. If so, this consistency places limits on the amount of influence the educational system can have. If someone's career plans have not changed, his exposure to various educational experiences has obviously not changed them. On the other hand, some educational experiences will almost automatically produce changes in career plans.

Within the limitations posed by the stability of career plans, it will be possible to ascertain the effects of a man's college and graduate school experiences on his career plans and his actual occupational attainment. Does getting good grades tend to encourage someone to raise his occupational sights? Do poor grades have the opposite effect? How important for occupational success is enrollment in graduate school or earning an advanced degree?

We need only remember that certain professions require higher degrees to see why aspirants who have not been able to get such degrees might decide to abandon plans to be in such professions. Also, continuance in professional training may provide a momentum of its own. After a certain point, it may become very difficult to abandon a substantial investment of time and money.

DETERMI-NANTS OF OCCUPA-TIONAL ATTAINMENT The variables to be used in this analysis start with parental SES and the person's own ability. The quality of the college from which a man graduated and prestige expectations are added next, followed by college grades, senior prestige expectations, the number of years during which a person was enrolled in graduate or professional school, the prestige associated with the occupation he expected three years out of college, the earning of a higher degree between 1964 and 1968, and the prestige of the occupation in which the person was actually engaged during 1968.

Though the number of variables makes the process seem somewhat long and rather complicated, the variables can be divided into two groups that help to keep things straight. The first group contains those variables related to career consistency, the prestige expectations. For the most part the remaining variables describe a man's progress through the higher educational system. The way the two sets interpenetrate is one of the primary concerns of this chapter. Parental SES and intellectual ability will be regarded as initial conditions for the two parallel causal systems.

In terms of temporal ordering, the first three variables refer to the socioeconomic status of the parents. The fourth, intellectual ability, is of obvious relevance to the process of occupational achievement. The most prestigious occupations are quite intellectually demanding. Though these variables are rather important in the general population, their effects will seem to be rather slight when educational attainment is controlled as rigorously as it is among a sample of college graduates. The measured effects of these variables will consequently be rather weak in this sample, even when a composite measure of SES is used.

		Standard	Weighted
Variable	Mean	deviation	N
Father's occupation	44.4	14.0	19,247
Father's education	12.2	3.3	19,256
Parental family income*	96.7	60.8	18,025
intellectual ability †	5.9	2.6	699
College quality	55.5	9.4	19,734
Freshman prestige expectations	64.9	9.2	17,253
College grades ‡	4.9	1.5	19,415
Senior prestige expectations	63.1	11.2	19,513
Years in graduate school	1.2	1.2	19,734
1964 prestige expectations	63.6	12.6	19,280
Higher degree since 1964§	.5	.8	4,419
1968 occupational prestige	60.4	12.2	4,425

TABLE 81 *Univariate statistics for variables used in analysis of men's prestige expectations*

*In hundreds of dollars.
†In deciles.
‡A+ and A = 9, B+ = 8, C− = 2, D+ or lower = 1.
§Bachelor's = 0, master's = 1, professional or doctoral = 2.

On the average, male 1961 college graduates came from families earning nearly $10,000 per year; their fathers were high school graduates and had an average prestige score of 44 (Table 81). Such a score is assigned to occupations such as insurance agent, real estate agent, bookkeeper, and foreman, and to certain skilled occupations such as electrician and machinist. In general, these are lower-middle- or upper-lower-class occupations.

The intellectual ability scores come mainly from college entrance tests and have been converted to deciles of the 1952 American Council on Education (ACE) test. The value of 6 indicates that college graduates are a little brighter than college entrants, for whom the mean score would be 5.

College quality is measured by Astin's (1965) "selectivity." The mean of 55.5 has no intrinsic meaning. This value corresponds to scores given many state universities, though the best public institutions score somewhat higher, and the best private colleges score higher still. Astin's measure was calculated in such a way that it would have a mean of 50 and a standard deviation of 10. The reason for our higher value is that Astin's computations were done with colleges as the unit and ours were done with graduates

	Father's education	Parental family income	Parental SES*	Intellectual ability	College quality
TABLE 82 Correlations between variables used in analysis of 1968 occupational prestige (Pearson r) Variable					
Father's occupation	.59	.42	.22	.24	
Father's education		.44	.26	.30	
Parental family income			.18	.33	
Parental SES			.28	.37	
Intellectual ability				.31	
College quality					
Freshman prestige expectations					
College grades					
Senior prestige expectations					
Years in graduate school					
1964 prestige expectations					
Higher degree since 1964					

*Correlations between parental SES and the other variables are the multiple correlations of father's occupation, father's education, and parental family income with these variables.

†Estimated from other correlations.

as the unit. Since there are more people in the big schools than in the small and since obscure small schools get low scores, a measure calculated on students will necessarily be higher than one calculated on schools.

Male alumni had college grades that averaged almost exactly B—, or 5 on this scale. On the average, they had been enrolled in graduate or professional school during one and a quarter academic years. The "average" higher degree earned indicates that most men in the sample had not yet achieved a master's degree. The period covered by this item, 1964 to 1968, was chosen to minimize the redundancy between enrollment and degree earning and to allow both to be placed unambiguously in a causal model.

These male alumni expected to enter occupations with prestige scores ranging from 63 to 65. Such scores are received by occupations such as federal public administrators, various natural and

Freshman prestige expectations	College grades	Senior prestige expectations	Years in graduate school	1964 prestige expectations	Higher degree since 1964	1968 occupational prestige
.13	.03	.10	.14	.10	.12	.06
.15	.04	.10	.16	.10	.17	.08
.09	−.03	−.01	.10	−.00	.13	.00
.16	.07	.13	.17	.13	.18	.10
.22	.34	.23	.23	.21	.21†	.20†
.17	.02	.10	.15	.09	.17	.17
	.12	.48	.31	.33	.27	.32
		.28	.31	.26	.26	.26
			.48	.58	.35	.46
				.53	.57	.48
					.40	.60
						.42

social scientists (if they are not college professors), and high school teachers—by occupations that are clearly professional but not the topmost professions like medicine, college teaching, or law, which score 82, 78, and 76, respectively. The mean score on 1968 prestige is 60, only slightly lower than the average expectation score.

The rather close correspondence in mean scores of 1964 prestige expectations and 1968 prestige (64 to 60) is encouraging evidence that the expectations are not wildly unrealistic.

The remaining information needed for the analysis that we shall report here will be supplied by the correlations between all the variables used. These are given in Table 82.

A few words about the relations shown will be useful, but the actual analysis will cover their importance, and detailed discussion will be postponed until then. It will be helpful to divide the 12 variables into three groups: family background (father's occupational prestige and education, plus parental family income), academic performance (academic ability, college quality, college grades, years in graduate school, and highest degree), and prestige expectations and attainment.

Starting at the beginning, we see that the three family background variables are rather highly related. The correlation of .59 between father's prestige and education is higher than the value for all men in the general population, but in occupations held by fathers of college graduates, educational requirements are relatively rigorous. Physicians need M.D.'s, schoolteachers and engineers need bachelor's degrees, as do many businessmen. Such requirements could account for the relatively high correlations found in our sample. The other correlations between parental income, education, and occupation are quite respectable, as they should be. Since the three variables are the chief sociological measures of socioeconomic status, they should be related, and they are. This analysis will combine these three variables into a single measure of parental SES, arrived at by regressing all other variables on the three indicators. This procedure maximizes the linear combination of each of the three variables with all the others. The entries for the correlations of SES with other variables are simply the appropriate multiple correlation coefficients.

Note that SES and college quality are moderately related. For the most part, this correlation reflects the fact that well-to-do parents can afford to send their children to better schools. Intellectual ability is moderately related to parental status. College grades, on the other hand, are basically unrelated to parental SES. How well a man does in college, if he graduates, is not related to the socioeconomic circumstances of his childhood. Enrollment in graduate school is weakly related to family background.

More important are the small relations between parental background and the son's own prestige expectations. Here is another good place to remember that we are dealing with college graduates and that comparisons with the total population are meaningful only when education is controlled.

The relations of the academic performance variables are pretty much what one might expect. The correlations between ability and college quality and between ability and grades (.31 and .34, respectively) simply indicate that bright men graduate from good colleges and that they tend to get good grades. The negligible relation between grades and college quality means that American colleges grade on the curve—at least they did in 1961 and before. With grading standards set by each institution, a sizable correlation between grades and quality is impossible. Grades seem about twice as strongly related to graduate enrollment as is college quality.

The academic performance items are, on the whole, quite respectably related to prestige expectations, with selectivity being the weakest of the lot. The stronger correlations between grades and later career expectations, compared to freshman expectations, may indicate some selection during college, with the better students entering the high-prestige careers and the poor ones entering the lower-prestige careers. This seems particularly true in light of the constancy of the correlations between ability and prestige expectations. The correlation of .53 between years in graduate school and prestige expectations held three years after graduation (1964) exaggerates the effects of the former on the latter because seniors aiming for high-prestige careers were likely to go to graduate school. Even so, the direct effect of enrollment on prestige is substantial.

For the most part, actual 1968 occupational prestige is related to the other variables in much the same way as are prestige expectations. This is an encouraging clue that the expectations really do predict the reality. Further evidence to this effect is the correlation of .60 between 1964 prestige expectations and 1968 prestige. The correlation overestimates the independent effects of the expectations, but analysis reveals them to be quite large.

This completes the preliminary review of the basic data used in the analysis of prestige expectations. The first problem we shall discuss is the relation of freshman prestige expectations and college quality to the initial variables.

PRESTIGE EXPECTATIONS As the reader will remember from the explanation of path analysis in the preceding chapter, this method ordinarily demands that all variables but the initial ones be unambiguously ordered in time. This requirement comes about because it keeps the algebra neat; the proper direct and indirect paths sum to the value of the appropriate zero-order correlation only if a true path coefficient links all but the initial variables. Fortunately, there are ways around this requirement, because the next two variables in this analysis should really be treated as contemporaneous. The fact that one can think of reasons why prestige expectations dating back to the freshman year in college might precede the quality of the college from which a person graduates and vice versa means that no unambiguous ordering of the two can be postulated.

Another way of looking at the technical problem is to note that, in a path analysis, one must be able to trace a path from each variable to all others. There must therefore be a numerical value, either a direct path or a set of indirect paths, linking each variable to all others. The two ways around this problem are (1) to treat each contemporaneous variable as a cause of the other, with arrows running in both directions, or (2) to treat the two variables as basically uncorrelated, when the causes of the two are taken into account. The latter has been chosen as the solution to this particular problem. It implies that the direct connection between the two variables is zero.[1]

The rather strange protuberance at the bottom of Figure 2 is a way of expressing the extent to which the relation between freshman expectations and college quality is explained by parental SES and intellectual ability. But first, let us look at the explanation of each variable taken singly. As far as freshman prestige expectations are concerned, ability's path coefficient is twice that of parental SES. This means that ability independently explains 4 percent of the variance and SES 1 percent. (These values are the squares of the two path coefficients.) In other words, the former is four times as strong as the latter, not twice as strong as the path coefficients would seem to indicate. On the other hand, SES is stronger than ability as a predictor of the quality of the college from which a man graduated. In the calculus of explained variance, parental SES is nearly twice as strong as ability. The major reason why SES is so powerful is that good colleges are expensive colleges. The ability of parents to pay high tuitions is therefore of considerable help in getting and keeping a young man in an elite college.

The two initial variables together explain relatively little of the variance in the two later ones, as the residual paths indicate. Ninety-four percent of the variance in freshman expectations remains to be explained, as does 81 percent of the variance in college quality.

We may now turn to the protuberance. At the end of the arrows are the values of the residual paths mentioned above. Linking the two arrows is a double-headed path indicating that no causal

[1] This approach is discussed by Duncan (1966) and Duncan et al. (1968, pp. 33–43).

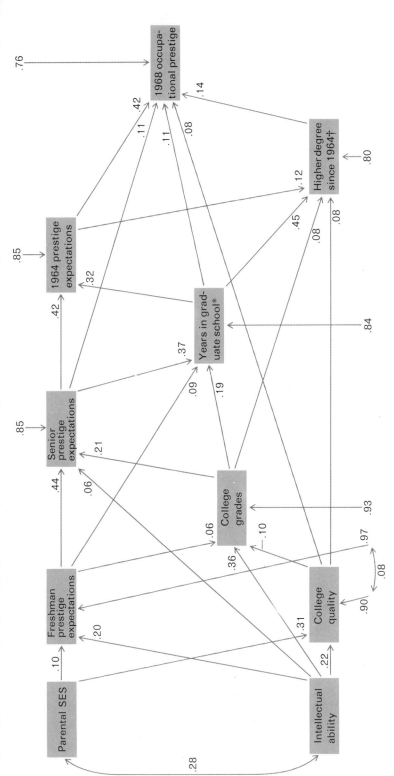

*All values < .08 in regression of Years in graduate school on Parental SES, College quality, College grades, and Freshman and Senior prestige expectations not shown.

†All values < .08 in regression of Higher degree on College quality, College grades, Freshman prestige expectations, Years in graduate school, and 1964 prestige expectations not shown.

FIGURE 2 *Path diagram relating prestige of job held in 1968 to earlier educational experiences and prestige expectations. Male college graduates only.*

direction is assumed between these two variables. The value of .08 indicates the extent to which the original zero-order correlation of .17 is *not* accounted for by the two prior variables. This path has two equivalent technical interpretations. It is the correlation between the residuals brought about because the relation between freshman expectations and college quality, net of SES and ability, is greater than zero. It is also the partial correlation between expectations and quality, controlling for parental SES and intellectual ability.

It is possible, by introducing appropriate correlations from the Project Talent data analyzed in Chapter 8, to reduce this partial correlation to zero. (These correlations were computed on data pertaining to men attending accredited four-year colleges in the year following high school graduation.) The two variables needed to supplement the original ones were high school senior prestige expectations and high school grades. The resulting set of four variables reduced the partial correlation between freshman expectations and college quality to .00. In other words, parental SES, ability, high school grades, and high school senior prestige expectations completely account for the relation between prestige expectations held during the freshman year in college and the quality of the college from which a male respondent graduated.

The Project Talent variables will be dropped from the remainder of this analysis for want of other necessary correlations. This is the reason why they were not included in Figure 2.

The next step in the analysis involves the determination of a man's college grades. Grades represent, of course, the student's formal academic record—the reports of his faculty members on how well he did in college. Presumably an able student in a demanding field will be persuaded by high academic performance to stay in his field—or in one about as demanding. A low-performing student may be influenced by his grades to decide that he would be better in a less demanding field.

Before looking at the effects of grades on other variables, let us ascertain the extent to which they are determined by the four earlier variables. Note first that there is no direct path linking parental SES and college grades. In this particular case, this omission is no more than a reflection of the fact that the two variables are not highly related at the zero-order level, as the correlation of .07 attests. To estimate the simple correlation by the direct paths and the correlations between independent variables in the diagram and SES, one would use the following formula:

$$r_{SG} = p_{GQ}r_{GS} + p_{GA}r_{AS} + p_{GF}r_{FS}$$

where S is parental SES, G college grades, Q college quality, A ability, and F freshman prestige expectations. The value given by this computation is .08, compared with the observed value of .07. There may be a slight negative relation between grades and parental affluence when the other three variables are controlled (.07 $-$ .08 $= -$.01), but it is really not worth taking into account.

Of the three variables whose direct effects are reported, only ability is strongly related to college grades. Since this link merely means that bright students got better grades than did dull students, it is no occasion for surprise. The path from freshman prestige expectations is small enough to be ignored. The $-$.10 linking college quality to grades is rather interesting. It comes about because colleges grade on the curve; as we have seen, the correlation between grades and college quality is practically zero. Given the other correlations among these variables, the negative net effect of college quality follows immediately. If two people with equal ability attend colleges of different quality, the person going to the better school will get poorer grades (Davis, 1966).

The value of the residual (.93) associated with the arrow originating outside the model indicates the size of the path coefficient needed to account for all the remaining variance. The variables in the model explain 13 percent of the variance.

One way of assessing higher education as a sorting device might be to examine the effects of academic performance on such things as career decisions. If it could be shown that the colleges sort the best students into the most demanding occupations, one could conclude that they are operating effectively as academic sorting agencies. Such a conclusion would, however, have to be hedged about with a veritable battery of qualifications, a few of which follow. In the first place, college grades are not particularly reliable measures—two faculty members can give, and have given, different grades to the same piece of work. Even if grades were completely reliable within a college, they would have to be adjusted to be comparable across institutions. An A from Harvard denotes a higher level of achievement than one from Boondocks Normal, as everyone knows.

Furthermore, it is not at all clear how desirable completely effective sorting would be. To raise the issue brings us to the edge of one of pedagogy's denser thickets, which we shall promptly skirt. Faculty members reward excellence and try to do so as objectively as they can. In informal counseling, they will try to steer students away from careers that will be too hard for them and encourage the bright ones to go to graduate school. But to dictate rather than to guide is an odious course. At some point a person's freedom of choice must be respected, and this may entail letting him make his own mistakes — staying in a career track too hard for him or continuing on a course that, by some abstract standard, may be a "waste" of his talents. All these reasons indicate why the relation between grades and prestige expectations may seem relatively weak.

The value of the direct path from grades to senior prestige expectations, .21, is respectable even though it is only about half of that from freshman to senior expectations (.44). The latter merely indicates that prestige expectations are rather stable during the college years. The fact that the path from grades is not negligible means that one reason men change their career intentions is their academic performance. Apparently the men getting the good grades raise their aspirations and those getting the poorer ones lower theirs.

Note that there is no direct path connecting college quality and senior prestige expectations. As we shall see later, this means that college quality is not very important; the relevant zero-order correlation of .10 expresses the magnitude of its effects.

The direct effects of grades on senior expectations (.21) represent most of the effects of this variable. The simple correlation is .28. (Indirect effects are given by the difference between the simple correlation and the direct path.) Most of the indirect effects result primarily from the compound path linking ability to grades and grades to senior expectations. It should be noted that this and all other indirect effects show how the impact of grades is spuriously inflated owing to its association with earlier causes of senior expectations.

As noted earlier, a postbaccalaureate degree is necessary to gain full standing in most of the occupations given highest prestige in our society. Looking forward, we may note that someone who expects to be in an intellectually demanding, and therefore prestigious, occupation needs to undertake advanced training. Looking backward, it is clear that a person who expected to be in such an occupation as a senior must have enrolled in graduate or professional school in order to carry out his intentions. As Figure 2 shows, the chief direct determinant of postbaccalaureate enrollment is senior prestige expectations, with a path coefficient of .37. This is twice as great as the .19 linking grades to years in graduate school. The reader should remember that the ratio of the proportion of variance accounted for by the two variables is given by the square of the two numbers (.14:.04). The better-qualified students are more likely to attend graduate school than are others; but even independently of one's qualifications, one's career intentions are the most important determinant of whether one goes or not.

Results with regard to freshman prestige expectations are rather interesting. That somewhat more than a fourth of this variable's effects are direct (.09/.31 = .29) does not indicate that it is unimportant. The path from freshman through senior prestige expectations to years in graduate school (.44)(.37) = .16 is nearly twice as large as the direct path, and together the two account for most of the freshman effects. The indirect effect indicates that much of the freshman effect is transmitted through senior expectations. In other words, it comes about through persistence in career plans. The causal model presented here means that the direct path does *not* represent persistence. Even if freshmen with high expectations changed to a less demanding career line, they were still somewhat likely to attend graduate school, even when academic performance was held constant.

The direct path from grades to years in graduate school represents about two-thirds of the former's total impact on the latter. Much of the remainder comes from the indirect path linking grades, senior expectations, and years in graduate school. Good grades help account for the senior pursuit of elite careers and are thereby further linked to graduate enrollment. The absence of a direct path from college quality is a mark of the rather trivial importance of this variable as a predictor of enrollment in graduate school. Net of ability and freshman expectations, its independent contribution is only .06.

The four determinants of years in graduate school account for 26 percent of the variance. In evaluating this figure, we should remember that an important determinant of graduate school attendance has been held constant instead of being left free to vary. As other research on this sample has shown, men are much more likely to undertake advanced education than women (Spaeth, forthcoming, Ch. 5). In other words, inclusion of sex as a variable would have increased the proportion of variance explained.

Though path diagrams seem to become more complicated as more variables are introduced, we have actually reached the simplest part of the one shown in Figure 2. Note that only two arrows lead to 1964 prestige expectations, the next step in the process. These two arrows originate in the two variables temporally closest to these expectations: years in graduate school and senior prestige expectations. As the path coefficients indicate, persistence in prestige expectations is the stronger of the two variables, with a direct path of .42, compared to that of .32 from years in graduate school. In the limited three-variable model being discussed here, all the effects of senior expectations are independent ones, because the indirect path going through years in graduate school indicates one way in which the influence of senior expectations is brought about. It reflects the extent to which vocational preparation as embodied in graduate training is part of the carrying out of senior prestige expectations.

The direct path from years in graduate school to 1964 expectations accounts for all its independent effects. The remainder is spuriously brought about by the fact that men who, as seniors, expected to be in prestigious careers also undertook advanced studies, whereas those who expected to be in lower-ranking occupations did not.

What does it mean that all four prior variables in this system can be ignored? Are they irrelevant or unimportant? Why go back before the senior year when an adequate explanation of 1964 prestige expectations can be constructed using data pertaining to 1961 or later? One way of answering these questions is to contrast two different kinds of analysis, the predictive and the analytic. From the predictive point of view, only senior expectations and years in graduate school are needed to account for 1964 expectations. All other variables are so much excess baggage. From the analytical point of view, however, all variables included in the model are pertinent because each contributes to a description of the process by which prestige expectations are formed and occupational allocation is accomplished

To see how important a variable is in a causal process, one must assess its independent contribution to a dependent variable. One way of doing this is to add all nonspurious indirect paths to the direct path. Another is to perform a multiple regression with all intervening variables omitted. In our model the variables influencing the direct contribution of freshman prestige expectations to the explanation of those held in 1964 are intellectual ability, parental SES, and college quality. Net of these variables, the freshman effects are substantial, with a value of .3. The net impact of ability is respectable, .14, and that of college quality is nil. These three variables explain 13 percent of the variance; ultimately 41 percent is explained. To carry the matter one step further, we may note that the independent effect of grades, net of ability, college quality, and freshman prestige expectations, is .2, a rather respectable value. The notion that college grades have nothing to do with occupational attainment is due for some revision.

OCCUPA-TIONAL ATTAINMENT SEVEN YEARS AFTER GRADUATION Now we may turn to the ultimate dependent variable in the model: the prestige of the occupation actually held by men working in 1968. Though the attainment of a higher degree is the next step, we shall not devote much space to this variable. Its path to 1968 occupational prestige of .14 indicates that it is not very important even though it is too large to be legitimately dropped from the model. The primary determinant of higher degree attainment is enrollment in graduate school in 1964 or before with 1964 prestige expectations also making a moderate contribution. It should be noted that while enrollment and degree attainment measure essentially the same thing, they are temporally independent. Enrollment covers the period from graduation to spring or summer of 1964; degree attainment covers the period starting with January, 1965. Hence, enrollment under this definition is not literally a necessary condition for degree attainment. The important fact to be noted, however, is the latter's relative lack of efficacy as a predictor of occupational attainment.

The relation between prestige expectations held at two points in time has been treated as a matter of simple persistence. The relation of expectations to reality raises a new question: Did what these male college graduates *think* they would be doing have any relation to what they actually *did*?

By far the most powerful predictor of the prestige of a man's actual occupation in 1968 is the prestige of the occupation that four years earlier he said he expected to hold. This may come as a surprise to a few skeptical social scientists who feel that you cannot trust what someone tells you, but it will not be much of a surprise to the rest of us. Exactly the same thing was true of enrollment in graduate school (Miller, 1963; Spaeth, forthcoming, Ch. 5). Young men who have graduated from college have a pretty good idea of where they are headed.

In fact, the only really important direct determinant of occupational attainment is occupational plans held four years earlier. The other variables in the model make much smaller contributions, the largest of which is associated with degree attainment, though the one for graduate enrollment is nearly as big. The path from senior prestige expectations indicates that an early decision may have small delayed effects. With the exception of this variable, the small direct paths are more tantalizing than substantively interesting. The indirect path leading from years in graduate school through 1964 expectations to occupational attainment has a value of .14, which is larger than that of the direct path. What are the independent contributions of the variables in the system?

Before answering this question, it will be necessary to get a few technical details out of the way. For one thing, an explanation of why tests of statistical significance have not been used seems to be in order. The measure of intellectual ability used here was collected on 6 percent of the total sample of graduates. Names of 10 percent of the total sample were sent to registrars with requests for college entrance examination scores in hopes that the relatively small number of individuals per school would encourage administrative cooperation. Scores were returned for 60 percent of this subsample, with missing data coming about primarily because some institutions did not require such examinations or failed to keep records for a long enough period. Analyses in which ability is an independent variable should be viewed as based on the 699 cases provided by this subsample. Ability enters directly only in the analysis of grades and senior prestige expectations. Ability's effects on grades are more than large enough for statistical significance, but its effects on senior expectations are not significant. The same is true of the negative direct path from college quality to grades. The important fact about these paths is not that they fall short of statistical significance but that they are small. In all analyses where ability does not enter directly, virtually any path reported will be statistically significant because the number of cases is so large. In fact, we have ignored many significant but small direct paths in the construction of Figure 2. In an analysis of this type, one wants substantively interesting correlations to be significant. With the possible exception of the path from college quality to grades, this is the case.

The same problem is raised in somewhat different form by the last two steps in this analysis. The 1968 data come from a sample that included nearly 3,100 males but in which ability scores were so infrequent as to be not worth computing. The correlations of ability with degree attainment and with occupational attainment have been estimated from the other correlations in a manner similar to that discussed on page 159. The N for these correlations must therefore be considered as approximating 3,000 cases, but the reader should understand that the size of the relationship is probably underestimated. Nevertheless, the values of the two correlations are quite reasonable. That between ability and degree attainment is .21, which compares with the .23 between ability and years in graduate school. Similarly, the estimated correlation between ability and occupational attainment is .20, compared to .21 between ability and 1964 prestige expectations. It seems unlikely that the estimates are off by much.

We may now turn to a discussion of the independent contribution of each prior variable to the explanation of 1968 occupational attainment. Correlations of ability with higher degrees earned and occupational prestige were estimated from other correlations in the model. The relevant data are presented in Table 83, which shows the independent effects of each successive new variable. In the first column are the effects of the two initial variables. In the second is the nonspurious contribution of the next two variables, net of the initial two and of each other. In the third is the contribution of grades, net of the first four variables. The coefficients involved are simply direct paths in successively more elaborate models. The fourth column shows the effects of senior expectations, net of its five predecessors, and so on to the last column, which recapitulates the data in Figure 2.

The impact of intellectual ability is not negligible. Independent of parental SES, the path of .19 indicates that ability explains 4 percent of the variance in the occupational attainment of college graduate males. Parental SES, on the other hand, has only trivial effects, as the path of .04 indicates. The reader should recall that Chapter 8 demonstrated a strong linkage between parental SES and college attendance. Given the fact that someone is a college

TABLE 83 *Total independent effects of various variables on 1968 occupational prestige (Standardized net regression weights)*

Variable	Independent effects of added variable						
	Parental SES and intellectual ability	College quality and freshman prestige expectations	College grades	Senior prestige expectations	Years in graduate school	1964 prestige expectations	Higher degree since 1964
Parental SES	.04	—.02	—.02	—.03	—.05	—.06	—.06
Intellectual ability	.19	.12	.04	.02	.01	.00	*
College quality		.10	.12	.12	.10	.11	.10
Freshman prestige expectations		.28	.27	.12	.09	.08	.07
College grades			.21	.13	.08	.06	.05
Senior prestige expectations				.35	.24	.08	.07
Years in graduate school					.29	.16	.10
1964 prestige expectations						.43	.42
Higher degree since 1964							.13
R^2	.04	.13	.17	.26	.32	.43	.44
R	.21	.36	.41	.51	.56	.65	.66

*Since the correlations of intellectual ability with higher degree since 1964 and 1968 occupational prestige were estimated on the basis of the other variables listed in this column, ability's direct path will necessarily be 0 in the model including all other independent variables. It has therefore been omitted from the computations in the last column. It should be noted that the effects of ability are probably slightly underestimated throughout.

graduate, the social characteristics of his parents may be of little benefit in his occupational career, but they are not irrelevant to his being at such a favorable starting point.

By looking along the rows of tables like this one, it is possible to see how the effects of one variable on another are transmitted through intervening variables. Part of the ability effects are transmitted through freshman prestige expectations and college quality. An equally large part is transmitted through college grades.

As the next column of the table shows, college quality is a relatively minor determinant of the gross kind of occupational attainment denoted by prestige (Spaeth, 1968). It is interesting to note that its effects, small as they are, are not transmitted by later variables in the model. Evaluation of the path of .28 describing the non-spurious effects of freshman expectations must remain a little hazy. The interval between college entrance and 1968 is at least the 11 years starting in 1957. Is it remarkable that there is any carry-over between plans and reality over such a long period? Or is it, perhaps, a little surprising that male college graduates are no more consistent than this? We tend to lean slightly more to the former than to the latter view, but since there are no absolute criteria by which to substantiate such an opinion, it must remain only that.

There is a widely held view that academic performance is almost totally unrelated to success outside the academy, that grades are not related to occupational attainment. As Table 83 shows, however, this is not the case. The path coefficient of .21 indicates that grades have a substantial impact on the prestige of the occupation held by a man seven years after graduation. Note that the grades effect reported here is independent of the four earlier variables in the model, one of which is intellectual ability. As later variables are added to the model, the *direct* effects of grades diminish to a point where they need no longer be taken into account. This is only another way of saying that the later variables do a rather good job of explaining why grades have the impact that they do. It does not say that the importance of grades as a factor in the causal process is diminished.

The indirect effects of grades are primarily transmitted through senior prestige expectations and secondarily through enrollment in graduate school. The grades a man receives may prompt him to review his career decisions and to bring career plans into line with his academic performance.

Senior expectations make a rather strong independent contribution to occupational attainment, with a value of .35. Reading across the row, we note that the drop from .35 to .24 indicates that the impact of senior expectations on advanced education accounts for part of the indirect effects of the former. At the same time, the drop from .24 to .08 indicates that persistence in career plans is an even larger part of the indirect effects of this variable.

The years enrolled in graduate school through 1964 is a very respectable predictor of occupational attainment in 1968, with an independent contribution of .29. The role of advanced training as a means to professional standing is quite clear, with a substantial part of the indirect effects of enrollment coming from its impact on prestige expectations held in 1964.

The 1964 expectations make the strongest independent contribution to actual occupational attainment, as the coefficient of .43 indicates. The increase in the independent impact of expectations on reality as the former grow closer in time to the latter is only to be expected. The closer a person comes to performing a certain behavior, the more accurately will he be able to predict what he will do. In Figure 2, the path coefficients that lead from expectations held at one time to those held at the next and from 1964 expectations to actual 1968 prestige are remarkably similar in value. Expectations predict behavior about as well as they do each other.

SUMMARY The entire diagram is rather easily summarized. There are two interpenetrating causal systems, one involving career plans and the other involving academic or intellectual variables. Persistence in career plans is somewhat stronger than academic prowess or performance in explaining prestige expectations or attainment. But college grades and enrollment in graduate school modify prestige expectations, while at the same time being modified by them.

American higher education does tend to sort men into careers different from those they originally expected to be in, though it does not completely eradicate the effects of early choices. Whether the impact of a man's course through the higher educational system is considered too great or too slight depends on one's views on the desirability of academically related sorting. We shall have something to say about the social functions and dysfunctions of higher education as a sorting device in the concluding chapter.

Part Three
Conclusion

10. The Present State of Higher Education

The normal procedure for survey researchers, after they have presented their findings, is to fold their tables and quietly steal away, with the hope that their results will be of some help to the policy makers who commissioned the study. Many times the import of one's findings is rather ambiguous, with all the definiteness of an inkblot. Almost any reader of a research report can find somewhere in that report a table that will confirm his own biases and prejudices.

The authors of this volume have decided to depart from the traditional pattern and to state as forcefully and as vigorously as they can what they think the data in this volume mean and what policies and attitudes might be appropriate responses to the data. There are two reasons for such departure from approved norms:

1 The Carnegie Commission on Higher Education is not an ordinary client; it has been set up to make recommendations and is quite capable of accepting or rejecting recommendations made to it by others.

2 The present situation in American higher education is such that the normal antiseptic response to a survey research report does not seem to be an adequate response.

Much of this chapter will be based on alumni criticisms of higher education and our evaluations of them. But before turning to these criticisms, we shall deal with an issue for which behavioral evidence is more appropriate than is attitudinal. The last two chapters have shown that colleges and universities do operate as sorting and screening agencies. As they progress through the system, bright men, or those who perform well, tend to become more oriented to the most intellectually demanding occupations. The reverse is true of the men with poorer records.

To persons who have graduated in the late sixties, these findings might seem a criticism in themselves because they could be taken as evidence that higher education gives aid and comfort to the military-industrial complex. Since nearly all male alumni hold middle-class jobs, they almost necessarily make at least an indirect contribution to the maintenance of the military-industrial complex. This fact is much less a result of screening than it is of the lack of it. Most of the alumni in the class of '61 are in middle-class jobs because they want to be.

Allocation to different occupations indicates a greater degree of sorting. Men do change their career plans in response to their success or failure in college or graduate school, and the plans are important influences on the kinds of jobs actually held. The fact remains, however, that plans are a more important independent influence than academic performance. On the face of it, higher education is only a mildly effective screening device.

Should it be anything more? We are inclined to think not. The system as it now operates leaves considerable room for a man to change his mind about his plans while it formally influences his plans in only a minor way. We are certainly opposed to any form of coercion in this matter, and current campus politics makes even the semblance of coercion unwise.

Nonetheless, our findings on occupational choice indicate that higher education has some effects. What kinds of effects do its "products" want it to have? The alumni make rather stringent demands on the higher educational enterprise—parent, priest, psychiatrist, master craftsman, confidant, charismatic leader, prophet, social reformer—the college is expected to be all these. It is supposed to *do* something to the people who attend it. The alumni, of course, are not alone in these expectations for higher education; most other Americans and, one suspects, most educators have also expressed at least some of the same expectations at one time or another. It seems to us that it would be very desirable if a national consensus could be established that would not make as many demands of the college experience. We are not in agreement with those who argue that all we may expect of higher education is custody and screening, but neither are we willing to agree with those who think that it has failed if it does not produce lots of people with a degree of personal nobility never before seen on a mass basis.

Somewhere between screening and ennobling, we suspect, can be found a series of goals for higher education that are both feasible and challenging.

On the one hand, we agree with those psychologists who point out that the higher educational experience takes place at one of the most critical and most plastic periods in the human maturation process. One list of the major dimensions of development occurring during the college years includes the following: developing competence, managing emotions, developing autonomy, establishing identity, freeing interpersonal relationships, developing purpose, and developing integrity (Chickering, 1969). The fact that the young person is more or less consciously engaged in these activities must always be kept in mind by educators.

But colleges must also bear in mind that they are only one of many institutions with which the student is involved. They cannot expect to influence the totality of his life and should not endeavor to do so. They should even be modest enough to acknowledge that their influence may be much less decisive than that of his family, his friends, his sweetheart, and, quite possibly, the mass media. The fact that many of these other institutions have their influence on the young person in the same physical location where the higher educational enterprise operates has perhaps deceived us into believing that these institutions are also part of his higher educational experience. They are not. The experience, in its turn, influences them, but it would be naive of the educator to assume that he is going to have very much control over the impact these other institutions have on the personality development of his student.

The personality of the student, then, will develop or not develop rather independently of what his teachers do. For some students the intervention of the educator may be decisive; for others, it may be important, but scarcely decisive; and for yet others, it will be quite irrelevant. They will acquire certain skills and knowledge as a result of the higher educational experience, but their personalities will remain largely unaffected by much of it. Their autonomy, identity, integrity, etc., will be shaped by other institutions.

It therefore seems clear that at least at the present state of our ability to influence personality development, we should not be at all surprised that the values of students are relatively unaffected by higher education. On the contrary, one would be surprised if student values were much changed.

However, we think it is a very different thing to say that the college may not change values than to say that the college makes no contribution to the development of the human personality; for there is, we repeat, a middle ground between screening and molding personality.

In attempting to assess the proper role of higher education in individual development, the writers detected what seems to them to be a convergence in the thinking of three recent educational writers — Tussman, Schwab, and Katz. Tussman (1969) sees the first two years of college as essentially a philosophical and moral experience in which the young person seeks to clarify his values by wrestling with the various possible answers to certain critical questions. These two years of college, if we interpret him rightly, are spent in a search for a clearer and more specific meaning system or interpretive scheme. The quest is primarily intellectual, though the ethical issues discussed should have powerful emotional overtones and impact. The cognitive dimension of the personality cannot face critical issues of life in a state of aloof disinterest.

For Schwab (1969), higher education seeks to facilitate in the student the ability to consider alternatives and communicate toward consensus intelligently. Again the goal is primarily intellectual: the development of the cognitive habits that enable one to suspend judgment until one has considered the various sides of an issue and also to reserve the expression of one's opinion until one is able to state it in a way that is most likely to lead to mature collaboration with others.

Katz (1968) emphasizes the fact that the student is a developing human personality seeking self-awareness, competency, and interpersonal skills. The point that needs to be emphasized, it seems to us, is that the ability to consider alternatives intelligently, the ability to communicate toward consensus, and the ability to respond in an intelligent way to the critical issues of life are also developmental needs. Not only is there no conflict between Katz's developmental approach to education and Tussman's and Schwab's approach, but there is a necessary congruence between them. Tussman and Schwab are well aware that their goals respond to powerful, deep-seated emotional needs of their students — even if the students are not always aware of it. And Katz, on his part, seems equally well aware that cognitive development is among the most critical developmental tasks that the late adolescent faces.

Of course, cognitive development has traditionally been one of education's primary concerns. Furthermore, our alumni seem to be criticizing their colleges chiefly on the grounds that they did not contribute enough to value formation or to the ability to form and express opinions intelligently. Schwab, Tussman, Katz, and the class of '61 seem to come rather close to echoing one another's opinions.

The relevancy of Katz and the rest of the developmental school of higher education is not that they provide an alternative to the intellectual goals advocated by men like Tussman and Schwab, nor that they have discovered that cognitive development is, in fact, a personality need. Their relevancy lies in the fact that awareness of the late adolescent developmental process can be helpful in facilitating intellectual development in the student. We think the class of '61 would say, "Why, of course!"

We are arguing that the student is neither all intellect nor all emotions but a complex combination of the two. The college should have an impact on the student's personality, but it should try to to do so largely through its facilitation of cognitive development, a facilitation that ought to take place in the context of a sensitive awareness of the developmental problems of the people with whom it is dealing. Alumni seem to be criticizing college experience on two counts: it did not contribute enough to their cognitive development, and it was not sufficiently aware of the personality development to which their intellectual training was supposed to contribute.

In connection with research on innovations in higher education, one of us has observed in action a program based on Tussman's approach. The strength of the program seems to be precisely its combination of values and intellect. Even though few of the philosophers discussed in the program were modern ones, the value issues were perceived to be thoroughly relevant. (It is hard to imagine the kind of horrendous antipedagogy that would be required to make *The Republic* seem irrelevant.) These issues were discussed in a context of serious intellectual analysis. In short, the issues were relevant, though ancient, and the materials were difficult. Students perceived both facts. As a result, they expressed such a sense of intellectual development that they said that they wanted to reread at the end of the year the work with which they had begun the year in order to be able to observe the development that had taken place in themselves.

It also seems to us that there are underlying similarities between the class of '61 and the class of '69. Our alumni are obviously a "cool" lot and rather square. Few of them have tried drugs, few have demonstrated, and about half are not in sympathy with the goals of the student protesters. But then, not very many members of the class of '69 have demonstrated, protested, or revolted, and various studies indicate that about half of them are not in sympathy with at least the tactics of student demonstrators. There has been some change, of course, since 1961: the protesting minority is larger and louder; the sympathetic moderates who agree with the goals but not the means of the protesters are significantly more numerous. Acceptance of the broader society is probably much smaller among today's graduates than among the class of '61 now or when they graduated. Still it is worth emphasizing that approximately half of the class of '61 do show sympathy with the protests and that the majority of them are willing to endorse at least some of the demands for student power. Furthermore, their responses indicate that they consider the value-formation dimension of higher education to be critical and that they are less than satisfied with the college's contribution to their intellectual and personality growth. Granting that they may have unrealistic notions about what colleges can accomplish, they still seem to want for their children the kind of college education that corresponds with the traditional humanistic version of higher education, and they want such an education because they think that this kind of education is the best preparation for later life. The 1961 alumni are rather quiet and dispassionate in stating such opinions; the 1969 alumni are neither quiet nor dispassionate.

The import of these criticisms, then, is not that higher education is too "intellectual" or too "psychological" but that it is not intellectual enough and not psychological enough, and above all, that it fails to see the essential links between these two dimensions of human personality growth.

We would argue, therefore, that American higher education would be well advised to reexamine the best of its own tradition in the light of contemporary psychological insights so that it may better do what it has been trying to do all along. The college that abandons intellectual goals may discover that its new goals are not only harder to achieve than the old ones but that the new ones are being achieved more effectively elsewhere.

We see at least two such temptations. The first is "relevancy." It is argued that education must be linked with life and that young people must therefore go where life is, either through work-study programs, through social action in the "inner city," or, finally, through viewing the college as essentially a social reform agency.

One can hardly argue that education must be linked with life, but one is inclined to suspect that an educational experience which does not persuade the students that life is to be found in the dormitories, classrooms, cafeterias, and quadrangles on their campus is not going to enable them to find life anywhere else. He who cannot discover and alleviate human misery when it is down the corridor from his room is not likely, in the final analysis, to learn much from the human misery in the inner city. Life is where one finds it; if one does not find it in one's present environment, there is no reason to expect that one will find it elsewhere.

We do not intend to attack work-study programs per se but simply to question the notion that they have any automatic educational value, much less that they necessarily bring higher education more closely into contact with life. Perhaps we are somewhat prejudiced because students from one such work-study program have worked as coders for the National Opinion Research Center. This is life?

Nor do we intend to criticize the involvement of students in social reform. Students are human beings, human beings have obligations to work for social reform, and therefore it is most praiseworthy for students to be engaged in such activities. But we do not think that a semester or a year in the inner city will automatically turn a young person into a more intelligent, sophisticated, sensitive social reformer. On the contrary, in some instances there is some risk that he may become a narrow, bigoted zealot whose superficial knowledge and skills, mixed with upper-middle-class guilt feelings, would make him the kind of romantic revolutionary who, in the final analysis, is an obstacle to social reform. We are not opposed to inner-city projects. On the contrary, one of us has strongly supported them for a number of years. But we are skeptical that they will automatically contribute to the intellectual development of the young person. For participation in work study, reform, or other kinds of amelioration will be educative only if the participant subjects his experience to a searching, intellectually based, analysis.

Finally, we are dismayed by the notion that the college itself should abandon its traditional intellectual goals and devote itself to the business of social reform. Few institutions can be more ill equipped to do the things needed to reform society. Most American higher educational institutions are barely able to tend to their own problems. When they presume that they can solve the whole of society's problems, they are engaging in a form of hubris that is an invitation to disintegration and destruction. The college can contribute to reforming society by educating young people who are committed to and skillful at social reform. Having failed to produce many such young people in the past, the college should not ask us to believe that it will now take up the job of reform. Persons who hold these views are saying, in effect: "We have failed at our main task, so now you must let us try something even more important." They should not be surprised that the rest of society reacts in a hostile way to such demands, for they are naive indeed.

The critical question that must be asked about any educational program is whether it facilitates the student's capacity for systematic thought, or, to use Schwab's (1969, p. 116) words, "intelligent consideration of alternatives and intelligent communications toward consensus." The inner-city programs may well be useful efforts for social reform—though one wonders how much students can do in the space of a semester or year to change anything in the inner city. Work-study programs may be essential to higher education, but unless the student grows in his ability to consider alternatives and communicate toward consensus, then, educationally speaking, work-study programs are a waste of time. Many such programs may be fun, they may be emotionally stimulating, they may be a welcome relief from the arduousness of study, but they are not education.

We are insisting, then, that however helpful such programs may be to the educational process, their impact is not automatic; an inner-city experience, for example, that is accompanied by careful reading of the relevant literature and by challenging questions from a faculty member who refuses to be satisfied with simplistic analyses and solutions can have immense educational value. But such reading and questioning require a great deal of skill on the part of those responsible for the program, and it runs against the grain of current students' romantic ideologies. Who needs to read? Who needs to consider alternatives? The answer to these questions, however unpleasant they may be to some young romantics, is, "Anyone who claims to have intelligence."

The second temptation to depart from the traditional cognitive goals of higher education is the T-group temptation. Having failed to facilitate, at least in a very impressive fashion, the cognitive development of its students, the college (at least if we are to believe certain educational experimenters) must now become a therapeutic institution. And therapy in this context means encounter groups, marathon groups, sensitivity groups, affinity groups, white and black caucuses, and could even embrace astrology, witchcraft, divination, contemplation, drugs, rock music, and the whole psychedelic bag. The emotions must be rubbed raw; students must go through a psychological pressure cooker; defense mechanisms must be stripped away; personality structures must be shaken up, if not destroyed; confrontation must become the order of the day; the college must "swing"; it must "turn on"; it must be "hip."

The college that assumes that it can become a "swinger" is about as attractive as a middle-aged matron who thinks that with the help of the right clothes, the right vocabulary, and the right drugs she can become a 17-year-old hippie. Even so, we may be in for a considerable amount of this psychological and psychedelic experimentation in higher education.

It is not our intention to deny that good higher education has a therapeutic component. Nor are we opposed to wide-scale experimentation with much closer communities of faculty and students than have been tried heretofore. We are inclined to be highly sympathetic toward such experimentation. Neither are we prepared to say that encounter sessions, *I Ching* groups, and even marathon therapy sessions do not have a place in American society and may not make a contribution to the personality-development of many young people. We are simply asserting that higher education has other things to do—things for which it has been explicitly established, and which no one else is able to do better or even claims to do.

One would scarcely want to deny that group-dynamic sessions with the right participants presided over by skillful psychologists can contribute to human growth, but the problem in much of the present enthusiasm for group dynamics seems to be that these sessions are intended for everyone, to be presided over by anyone, and as a substitute for almost everything else. Group therapy, however admirable, does not contribute directly to the development of man's power to consider alternatives or to communicate toward consensus. It may well facilitate both such endeavors; but a concern for process, however excellent, is no substitute for a concern about substance.

If we were asked to make a single recommendation on the basis of the data presented in the present study, it would be not that education hie itself into the inner city, nor that it create more work-study programs, nor that it establish marathon encounter groups on campus—though all these activities may be virtuous and praiseworthy—but rather that it concern itself more with the analysis and development of values, which is something rather different from "changing values."[1] The college's perceived contribution to value formation seems to be the strongest predictor of alumni satisfaction seven years after graduation. The case of the Catholic colleges is one which the rest of American higher education might consider. The Catholic colleges are criticized by their alumni both for the regulation of student life and for inferior academic quality. Yet despite this fact, these alumni are more loyal and more likely to say that they want their children to go to their colleges, precisely because of the contribution these colleges made to their value formation.

We do not condone rigid control of student life or support academic mediocrity. We are not proposing that consideration of values be substituted for academic quality or student freedom. Rather, it seems to us appropriate that a higher educational institution have both. Tussman, Schwab, and Katz all stress, each in his own way, the importance of the value-development dimension of the higher educational experience. Indeed, when one stops to consider, it is remarkable how little direct concern with values there is in most American higher education, despite the fact that many young people are intensely concerned—one might almost say driven—by value questions. In fact, on a priori grounds, one would expect serious dissatisfaction from people who come to an institution with value questions, wanting that institution to contribute to the resolution of these questions, and then discover that it reacts to the question of values in much the way that a Victorian spinster reacted to the question of sex.[2]

It is now time to consider some criticisms of our views, which are

[1] The former goal acknowledges that broad value frameworks for most have been fairly firmly established long before the young person comes to college and that what the college can do is to assist in the refinement, clarification, and analysis of these values. The latter assumes, we think, that the students come to college with the "wrong" values and that the college can provide them with the "right" values.

[2] Perhaps we could convert many academic departments of philosophy into museums of positivism and analysis, coin a new phrase for intelligent and cogent thought, and take it from the beginning of the twentieth century all over again. This is not advocacy of turning back the clock. It would be a profound mistake to believe that the history of ideas has been uphill all the way. For a similar view of philosophy and a cogent discussion of relevance, see Kaplan (1970).

hardly held universally. We shall do so by considering who our critics might be, starting with students. One kind of student who might be out of sympathy with our views is the vocationally oriented person who is the first member of his family to have attended college. He probably wants to be taught something that will directly prepare him for a job. He may live at home, and his parents may very much want him to learn something that is palpably useful. To him, a liberal education might look like the irrelevant vestiges of an elitist past. But vocational training may turn out to be next to useless. For one thing, on-the-job training is unquestionably more effective than academic vocational training in conveying the demands of a specific job. For another, changing technology will change occupational requirements so rapidly that the vocational training one receives in college will quickly become obsolete.

The problem here is to persuade such a student that the analysis and understanding of ideas may be more effective occupational preparation than something that seems more immediately relevant. Fortunately, a direct approach is probably not the way to go about demonstrating the usefulness of the liberal arts. If our limited observations of innovative programs are of any validity, such programs are a lot more fun than the traditional type of lecture course. How attractive to the typical undergraduate would a program of the Tussman variety be? We know of one such program with students of this kind; some of them are spreading the word about how much they like it.

New and old colleges are establishing programs oriented toward general intellectual issues. They seem to be attracting more students than they can handle. We know of no such program that does not have to turn applicants away. The signs here seem rather hopeful.

What about the other end of the educational spectrum? What about the intelligent but mindless barbarians who are such a visible fraction of the student bodies of elite colleges and universities? Not the least of this benighted group are the devotees of "feeling." They think that reason has had its chance and failed, that appreciation of subtlety and analysis of complexity are just establishmentarian cop-outs. These are just the kinds of skills that they need to learn. An ironic, if not very surprising, outcome of such learning might be the realization that they hadn't been feeling too well.

How could one arrange things so that such students might find this out? There are even signs of hope here. An increasingly prominent concern of many college students is the urgent question of environmental quality. If one moves beyond swearing at the evil polluters and attempts to do something about pollution, it quickly becomes apparent that the issues are complex and require considerable technical knowledge. This makes these issues a suitable basis for a curriculum. Moreover, pollution is nothing if not relevant. To try to do something about pollution requires understanding of the physical, biological, and social sciences. In addition, value questions would inevitably be of considerable importance in such a program. In this instance, the winds of fashion seem to be blowing in the right direction.

In fact, finding a student clientele for programs of the kind we are advocating does not seem to be a major problem. Such programs are attracting more candidates than they can admit, and they will probably continue to do so.

However, we do not want to advocate programs primarily designed for cognitive development to the exclusion of all others. One of the major strengths of American higher education is its diversity; this is a strength not to be sacrificed lightly. Even within this framework, there is room for attempts of the kind we advocate. Some young people come to college seeking occupational skills; others come seeking a passport to the upper middle class; still others seek maturity or excitement; and some come not quite sure why they have come. One of the more striking findings of the present study is that, seven years after graduation, many alumni are ready to pay substantial honor to the humanistic goals of education. Cognitive development will take one form for some students and quite another form for others. The setting in which such development takes place and the methods used by faculty members will differ from Harvard to a junior college. These differences are no reason for not attempting such education at both places.

It is clear from the above that a major problem in instituting such programs is presented by the faculty, though even here there are signs of hope. The most notorious of the faculty opponents of liberal education are those oriented to the attainment of recognition within their own disciplines. They strive for rather clear goals by means that are relatively easy to evaluate. In short, they are oriented to their professional peers who will pass judgment on their work and not to their own institutions or students. Such a professor feels that undergraduates are irrelevant and may be taught or not according to his whim or feelings of guilt. These men are the stars of academia, and we have no quarrel with them as such. They advance knowledge on its many frontiers, and this is no small part of the functions of a modern university.

We do quarrel with the notion that these men are the only appropriate models for other faculty members or for students. Let the scientific innovators continue as they are. Do not expect much in the way of undergraduate teaching from them. The problem is to make undergraduate teaching more attractive to less eminent scholars.

To some extent the solution to this problem may arise from the stratification of American higher education. The number of institutions accounting for the bulk of the doctorates in a given field are a small fraction of the total offering majors in that field or even of those offering the Ph.D. There seems to be evidence that some of the less eminent universities have abandoned their hopes of and efforts toward making themselves into instant Berkeleys. Furthermore, the payoff for a student who graduates from one of the elite institutions is not as great as most people seem to think (see Chapter 9). Instead of sending bright undergraduates to one of the elite knowledge factories, perhaps we should warn them off. There is a real danger that they will only become by-products in the knowledge factories and that they will be treated as such.

Of course, there are other faculty members who would take issue with our aims. For example, there are the faculty barbarians, who are the counterparts of the student barbarians. When one of the latter says, "Everything is feeling," or "The establishment is rotten beyond all hope," the former respond, "Yeah, man!" This is the ultimate pedagogical cop-out. How one is to teach members of a group to which one is earnestly striving to belong, we do not know.

Just as bad are the losers. They are the prophets of doom who see themselves caught between the student radicals on one side and the state legislators with their reactionary constituencies on the other. They expect the demise of American higher education by no later than the second quarter of next year. And there are the radicals who want to lose—who want to make matters worse so that the corruption of American society will be fully exposed and revolution can occur. Apparently the actions of the Weatherman faction of the SDS have shown the total futility of this posture. It seems to be less popular this year than last.

Unfortunately, the barbarians and the losers have found a common educational cause. The barbarians say that our heritage can teach us nothing, therefore forget it. The losers say that colleges cannot teach anything, so stop trying. Together they say that we should let the students do their own thing or that we should try to cultivate something other than the intellect. The outcome, as likely as not, is a nursery school for late adolescents.

As should be clear by now, we are not advocating one particular curriculum. We do not subscribe to the elitist notion that there are certain works that should be familiar to all educated men. The advantage of the classics, but no less of environmental problems, is that they pose important issues on a level that is not easy to understand. When a student perceives that he has come to understand more about such an issue, he will also perceive that he has accomplished something worthwhile. This should be the outcome of any developmental task. It is important that students be afforded the best possible opportunity to achieve their full intellectual potential and observe its development over time in ways that will demonstrate to the student himself his increased competence.

In conclusion, we must say that it is possible to find grounds for hope. The student barbarians seem to be drawing a somewhat smaller following. Other students are attracted to programs designed to aid in cognitive development, even though they are quick to detect signs of establishmentarian patchwork. In many colleges, older faculty members are discovering that the old lecture method is interesting neither to their students nor to themselves. They are also discovering that the administration is willing to let them try something else. Not all the current innovations will succeed, but there will be many more attempts in the future than there have been in the past. Moreover, the most recent generation of Ph.D's seems increasingly oriented to teaching and less oriented to the scholarly rat race.

Despite the current air of crisis in higher education, the financial aspects of which seem certain to get worse before they get better, American higher education may well be on the move. If the net direction of movement is not clear, this is no great loss. True diversity of purpose and approach instead of accidental diversity brought about by differences in clientele and failure to reach the pinnacle of elite university status is all to the good. The barbarians and the losers may yet be vanquished, though it will probably be the latter who put up the stiffest fight.

This is no time to say that the game is not worth the candle. We conclude, then, with the observations of two modern-day sages—Vince Lombardi, late of Green Bay and now of Washington: "The winning isn't everything, it's the only thing"; and Charlie Brown: "Winning isn't everything, but losing isn't anything."

Commentary

Although this is both a sociological and a statistical study, my comments will be devoted more to the conclusions than to the methodology, which I am not competent to judge. I am somewhat competent in the substance of the study since, for more than 20 years, I have met and discussed educational matters with tens of thousands of alumni all across the land. Here, too, my experience may be atypical because the alumni of the University of Notre Dame are extraordinarily loyal and deeply committed to its purposes, both intellectually and financially. During a good year, over 80 percent of them contribute to the university's alumni fund, generally about $2 million. Having this continuing stake, they are not at all bashful about voicing their concerns and criticism of what goes on in the university. The very day that I wrote these lines, I spent several hours with our national alumni board on campus discussing a wide variety of educational subjects that are of great concern to the members.

Despite this experience, it seemed to me that I should fortify my own judgments by enlisting those of our former alumni director, Mr. James E. Armstrong. For more than 40 years, the alumni body of the university was his very life. Beyond this, he was a former president of the American Alumni Council and was well known in the body of professional alumni directors. What I have to say, therefore, reflects many of his judgments as well as my own, although I find that generally we are in substantive agreement. I take this opportunity to thank Mr. Armstrong for his great assistance.

Now to the report. One might question at the outset what could be gained from a survey of the class of 1961, since higher education is in such an enormous state of flux and has been during the whole period of the sixties. I suppose the only answer the authors would give to this comment is the French phrase, *faute de mieux* — what other data are available if one wants to study alumni and their reaction to their education and to the institutions in which they received it? The Commission faced the same problem and was happy to be able to rely upon the continuing data of the class of 1961 which were available through previous studies of NORC. However, there is enough validity to the above query to remind ourselves that we are judging a moving stream, even though we focus upon one class.

One should perhaps also comment that the class of 1961 entered college in 1957 and found there campuses that had undergone complete transformation from the pre-World War II era. They found a seriousness and a maturity, a direct approach to career preparation and an urgency, as well as a devaluation of the extracurricular activities which had marked the prewar campuses. They found what they found without having undergone the experience of the previous climate that characterizes all older alumni. Most of all perhaps they found an academic and, indeed, a total permissiveness which had developed on the campus to meet the needs of mature postservice enrollments. This enrollment of veterans had practically disappeared (with the exception of a few Korean veterans), but the permissiveness remained, providing a new and unprecedented freedom for these teenage freshmen just out of high school.

It was in this transitional period that the social and political tendencies of the students took off in all directions, but the 1961 class was versed enough in tradition to doubt the extent of a new freedom. As a result they show in their own record only a 9 percent involvement in civil right activities, a 5 percent involvement in antiwar movements, and a 4 percent venture into drugs. So, while they fostered the climate to come, they had little warning of the extent to which their revolutionary ideology and the continuing campus permissiveness would affect their successors. It is obvious to even the casual observer today that activity in civil rights, involvement in antiwar movements, and the use of drugs have multiplied as much as tenfold on some campuses since 1961.

According to the survey, a recent Gallup poll reflected a public rejection of student social and political views and activities. Despite this, the educational faith of the class of 1961 is reflected in the desire of 93 percent to have their boys attend college (and 86 percent, their girls). Perhaps a distinction has to be found between the public's rejection, which stems from the surface evidence of student unrest and disturbance, and the concern of young alumni, who believe deeply in education even while showing no great enthusiasm for sending their children to their own colleges. Yet, there is a persistent personal attachment of the class of 1961 to their colleges, 27 percent of them characterizing this as strong and 59 percent saying that they liked their colleges. Only 1 percent actively disliked their college, although this percentage seems likely to be substantially increased in subsequent student generations, if I read students correctly today. Whatever else one says about the current students, they are certainly more passionate in their likes and dislikes than former generations of students.

The authors point out that the concern of these alumni of 1961 is for the quality of education rather than for a particular campus identity. They are concerned not so much over student disturbances as over the loss of identity and purpose, and about the nature of the institution. These problems they attribute to administrative and faculty influences, or to the lack of them.

Alumni interest is most often demonstrated by alumni support. There is some significance in the fact that 37 percent of the alumni in the study contributed to their colleges during 1967–68. This percentage is higher than the national average of about 25 percent. We should not be overly optimistic about this showing of the class of 1961. The 1961 aura of the campus is still strong, the consciousness of institutional problems related to increasing costs is very much alive, and the professional methods of enlisting alumni support are at new high levels. Perhaps we should look at the other side of the coin and realize that, of this class, 63 percent did not make even a small contribution. As one facing daily the problem of financing rising educational costs in an institution, I would like to stress that the problem of retaining young alumni support is a very crucial one.

The traditional loyalty and sentiment which were once enough to secure support are almost gone on many campuses. Many of the students enrolling today can take or leave the particular college in which they are enrolled. One finds parents, even though they might be very loyal alumni of a particular institution, exercising great care in allowing their children free choice of the campus on which they wish to study.

What is the reason for this dissipation of loyalty and commitment by alumni to their particular institutions? One reason certainly may be that there are very few teachers like Mr. Chips on the usual campus today. Modern faculty members tend to be competent in their own discipline and, to a large extent, the demands of that discipline and progress within it dictate the campus on which they serve. It has been noted in many other studies that modern faculty members have a disciplinary, rather than an institutional, loyalty. Modern faculty members are also much more mobile than in the past, and it is difficult for students to derive loyalty and institutional commitment from senior members of a community who do not show much of these characteristics themselves. It has also been noted that administrators today tend to reflect an image more as corporate head and mediator of conflicting academic interests than as scholarly ruler of a kingdom of knowledge. All these facts may mean that the alumnus of the future will contribute to an institution because of its competence rather than because of the persons who make up the faculty and administration. This may be increasingly true of institutions with a religious affiliation in which, increasingly, academic excellence seems divorced from religious relevance.

While there are exceptions to the above observations, it would seem from the study that they cannot be documented. It is not that the alumni resent the divorce of academic competence and religious relevance. Only 1 percent of the 1961 class described themselves as belonging to the New Left, but over 50 percent said that they were political liberals. This seems to be reflected in their attitude toward present student activities. Roughly half approved of student protests and of self-governance in student areas. The majority still felt, however, that students should not dictate general campus policy, especially on serious academic matters such as appointment of faculty and tenure. On the other hand, one might suspect some disaffection with the growing secularism that seems to characterize certain formerly quite religious campuses. This would seem to be reflected in the concern of many alumni for the inculcation of values as an integral part of the total education derived from the college or university. More of this later.

Quality seems to be the persistent message in the survey, taking precedence over traditional ties or the nature of the institution. Career training was important to the 1961 group, but I think is less so today because of the explosion of knowledge. (It is quite possible to teach the very latest information today and believe that it will not be at all relevant 10 years from now.) There is also, of course, disaffection with the establishment, with all its career implications in the field of the military-industrial complex. From the survey and from current trends, it would seem that the higher educational institution of the future would do well to stress high quality in a pattern of general and humanistic education if it wishes to maintain the continuing loyalty of its alumni.

There are several ways in which one perceives this concern for the quality of general and humanistic education. Chapter 4, "Memories of Alma Mater," uncovers a modern sentiment for alma mater, but a dissatisfaction with the attitudes and applications of the education received, as now perceived. To oversimplify, these alumni believe that the administration and faculty should have taught them then what they are just now thinking. They stress intellectual and value development without ruling out career training. They believe that the goal of the college should be to turn out a responsible citizen. They strongly believe that identifiable value formation would develop alumni attachment to the institution.

Quotations from the questionnaires would indicate a need for personalization beyond the classroom. One could derive from this aspect of the study some fear of computerization, and its analog, impersonalization, which are the national fears on many fronts. There is the further fear of the loss of alma mater identity. I believe that one can perceive the seeds of a growing thesis that, since career training is decreasingly effective in the face of the tremendous increase of knowledge, the college education of the future should help the student to form a sense of values and a responsibility for citizenship and should provide him with a broad, general, humanistic, and cultural base which might continue to grow if we understood, better than at present, the basic processes of learning and of higher education.

An Episcopal priest may well have put his finger on the major conflicts of this generation, with its shaping toward a career training vacuum, when he said it was regrettable that "college should be wasted on the age group dominated by passion." On the basis of the several applications noted above, higher education might well take a look at developing the *passion for learning* during this period of general passion; at providing, through continuing education, for the more effective total application of career-training and citizenship-responsibility curricula. Chapter 5, "Reform of Higher Education," would seem to endorse the above points. The alumni asked for more electives in the humanities and the fine arts. They urged the stimulation of different and unrelated reading on campus. They wanted more psychology and sociology courses so that they could better understand their fellowmen. Only about 10 percent would worry about grades. My general reflection is that the alumni are on very solid ground in making all these suggestions, and I regret that there is so little response to them in the curricula of higher education today.

There is a further suggestion that is worth underlining here. Sixty percent of these alumni favor some interruption in the formal college educational process, half between high school and college, and the other half preferring some time during the college years. Many educational philosophers have commented today upon the growing fatigue that students feel in the highly competitive system from kindergarten to Ph.D. Many of us have heartily endorsed the thought that at a certain point along the line, students would become better educated by leaving the whole system for a year or two and doing something which would require them to *give* rather than to *take*. In this endeavor, they would find out quickly their own deficiencies, the state of their values, the depth of their generosity or the lack of it, the realistic difficulties of introducing social change, and many other things of high educational value. If one could extrapolate from the experience of former Peace Corps volunteers, they would return to education with much more zest, with a deeper conviction about the necessity of competence for good performance in any field, and with a deeper realization of what education is all about. Once again, I believe that the alumni are on target with this suggestion.

The alumni are obviously very much concerned that education be a personal affair, with warm human relationships between faculty and students. Only this, they believe, can bring personal and individual development as a fruit of higher education. However, higher education is facing the dilemma of reconciling the size of the operation with personalization of the process.

A general bit of conflicting evidence seemed to emerge from the survey. In discussing the transition from high school to college, the view was expressed that college has produced more (1) independent, (2) tolerant, (3) open-to-new-experience, (4) less rigid, and (5) less prejudiced people. If this is true, one might conclude that the task of higher education is being fairly well done insofar as producing a generally educated individual who is interested in his fellowmen and the welfare of his society. However, the survey mentions an alternative view that the product has come closer to bland mediocrity and that colleges "have labored mightily to produce a swarm of gnats."

I would be inclined to question the "swarm of gnats" thesis since, while the beneficiaries of higher education in the past years may have marched to different drummers, they did indeed march. It was from our campuses that we drew the economic leadership which made us the resource nation of the world. It was also from the campuses that we drew the military leadership which won World Wars I and II against the most powerful, traditional military machines in the world. In a sense, the amateurs beat the professionals at a time when all the free world agreed that this victory was essential to the future of humanity. It was from the campuses that we drew the molders of the various uses of atomic power. It was from the campuses that we drew the brains that put men on the moon, a tribute perhaps not so much to the achievement itself as to the potentials it dramatized.

We have as well, through our higher educational system, offered more and better education to more citizens than any other nation in history. This, in turn, has made our broadly based citizen-democracy the number one political power of the world. These same campuses produced the leaders who have dominated the airwaves, the literature, the theater, the radio, and the television screens of the world, one might say for better or for worse, but not always for worse. It is dangerous to be too nostalgic about the past, but neither should we underestimate the underlying achievement of our colleges and universities. Concern for that achievement did not begin at nine o'clock this morning. As Mr. Armstrong reminds me, the story of the success of higher education has never been fully understood or completely told and, unless it is, the future of higher education may lose the substance of its heritage in the fear of its shadows.

Having made this point, I still insist that, looking ahead, we must more than ever before dramatize for the college student the sheer enjoyment of the mind at work in the many fields of the mind's endeavor. No matter what the future careers of our graduates, we need not fear their loyalty if the passion for learning was born on our campuses and has continued for their intellectual and moral betterment across all the years of their postgraduate experience. Wherever they go, there will be new and vital pressures upon them to continue in the knowledgeable pursuit of their businesses or professions, to keep up with the information, as involvement demands, in such fields as religion, education, communications, social sciences, government, and the fine arts.

The day will never come when these alumni will not have to be exercising priorities in their personal and societal lives, priorities that will reflect their very real values and the state of their comprehension of themselves, their society, and the world at large—despite the enormous changes taking place all around them. If we truly arm them to do that one task, then I think they will have found that ultimate quality which seems, on reflection, to be so important to them. They will also have found the element of value which is the most difficult of all to teach and perhaps cannot be taught except by example of those who man the educational endeavor. One might reverse the position and say, "Why should they be loyal to our institutions and continue to support them if they have not found in them the kind of quality and value and educational experience that was meaningful for the rest of their lives?"

One learns more of the authors of this report in the final chapter, "The Present State of Higher Education," than in all the foregoing chapters where they must remain strictly within the perimeters of the evidence at hand. In this final chapter, they allow themselves the liberty of speculation which indeed they might well do since they are closer than anyone else to the questions and answers of the survey and might well perceive interpretative shadings that indicate horizons beyond the cut-and-dried data. In any event, what I am saying is that survey researchers should be allowed to have their fun, too, even though that fun may have to take place on thinner ice than that of the preceding chapters. I was very happy to see Part 3 come along because they lost me on several occasions in Part 2, about which, you will perceive, I have had little if anything to say. This reflects, no doubt, a flaw in my own education.

I am in substantial agreement with what the authors have to say in the concluding chapter, both by way of diagnosis and prescription. They begin by calling for some kind of national consensus as to what a college really should do in its educational endeavor. They believe that somewhere between screening and ennobling persons there ought to be a series of goals for higher education that are both feasible and challenging.

I have a minor disagreement on their next point which lists the development occurring during college years as the following: "Developing competence, managing emotions, developing autonomy, establishing identity, freeing interpersonal relationships, developing purpose, and developing integrity." My point of disagreement is not that these are not indeed major dimensions of development. I disagree with their point that colleges and universities have very little to do with this development, which derives primarily from many other institutions, such as family, friends, mass media, etc. I would agree that this cluster of institutions has enormous influence on the development of the personality of the student; but I would take it to be a half-truth to say that higher education, with its proper purpose and identity, does not have distinct advantage in correlating with these other institutions and in making a conscious effort to influence the totality of a student's life.

This would be particularly true in a residential university, of course. While it is perfectly true that personality may or may not develop through the process of formal higher education, it would seem to me that there should be some conscious effort to influence this development within the totality of the institution. As indicated above, I believe there is a very special problem in the area of developing personal values, but a discussion of this would take us too far afield at the moment. One might say, though, in a peripheral way that if the class of 1961 felt that they were not given enough value formation, it may be that their colleges and universities failed to identify the student as a complex combination of intellect and emotion. Perhaps these institutions also failed to see the link between intellectual and psychological development. Failing this, of course, there will be no effort to gear the total educational endeavor of an institution to do anything related to value formation. One will either simply ignore the question or say it is not our concern.

In discussing theses of Tussman, Schwab, and Katz, the authors make some very cogent points. The first would be that the criticism of the 1961 alumni of their own education "is not that higher education is too 'intellectual' or too 'psychological' but that it is not intellectual enough and not psychological enough, and above all, that it fails to see the essential links between these two dimensions of human personality growth." The authors then take on two modern temptations: "relevancy" and the T-group approach.

A few sentences are very quotable in their attack on the temptation of "relevancy": "We are dismayed by the notion that the college itself should abandon its traditional intellectual goals and devote itself to the business of social reform. . . . The college can contribute to reforming society by educating young people who are committed to and skillful at social reform. . . . Work-study programs may be essential to higher education, but unless the student grows in his ability to consider alternatives and communicate toward consensus, then, educationally speaking, work-study programs are a waste of time. Many such programs may be fun, they may be emotionally stimulating, they may be a welcome relief from the arduousness of study, but they are not education."

With regard to the second temptation, the T-group approach, they are again eminently quotable: "Group therapy, however admirable, does not contribute directly to the development of man's power to consider alternatives or to communicate toward consensus. It may well facilitate both such endeavors; but a concern for process, however excellent, is no substitute for a concern about substance."

I believe that no one could put the case more succinctly than this. However, it still leaves us with the problem of what is the proper role of the institution of higher learning in today's society. This, indeed, is the central concern of the Carnegie Commission on Higher Education. The authors return to this task in a single recommendation based on this study. They indicate that the college and university should concern themselves more with the analysis and development of values, which is something rather different from "changing values." I would agree with the authors that this is a matter of central concern, at least on the basis of the data reported here from the graduates of 1961; but I should add that there are several other concerns, equally important and no less difficult to achieve. To specify them at this time would go beyond the purpose of this brief commentary.

I believe that all of us owe a debt of gratitude to the authors for carrying us this far and for leaving some still unexplored territory to be covered in further studies of the Carnegie Commission on Higher Education. The authors believe, contrary to their own critics whom they characterize as "the barbarians and the losers," that higher education does have a future. I was delighted to see them conclude on this note of hope which has been rediscovered today as the virtue most needed by all who face the problems and challenges and the opportunities of this great endeavor of higher education.

(Rev.) Theodore M. Hesburgh, C.S.C.
President
University of Notre Dame

References

Astin, Alexander W.: "Productivity of Undergraduate Institutions," *Science*, **136**:129–135 (April 13, 1962).

Astin, Alexander W.: "Undergraduate Achievement and Institutional 'Excellence,'" *Science*, **161**:661–668 (August 16, 1968).

Astin, Alexander W.: "Undergraduate Institutions and the Production of Scientists," *Science*, **141**:334–338 (July 26, 1963).

Astin, Alexander W.: *Who Goes Where to College?* Science Research Associates, Inc., Chicago, 1965.

Bell, Daniel: "Notes on the Post-industrial Society," *The Public Interest*, (6):24–35 (Winter, 1967), and (7):102–118 (Spring, 1967).

Bell, Daniel: *The Reforming of General Education: The Columbia College Experience in Its National Setting*, Columbia University Press, New York, 1966.

Blau, Peter M., and Otis Dudley Duncan: *The American Occupational Structure*, John Wiley & Sons, Inc., New York, 1967.

Chickering, Arthur W.: *Education and Identity*, Jossey-Bass, Inc., San Francisco, 1969.

Counts, George S.: "The Social Status of Occupations: A Problem in Vocational Guidance," *The School Review*, **33**:16–27 (January, 1925).

Davis, James A.: "The Campus as a Frogpond: An Application of the Theory of Relative Deprivation to Career Decisions of College Men," *American Journal of Sociology*, **72**:17–31 (July, 1966).

Davis, James A.: *Great Aspirations: The Graduate School Plans of America's College Seniors*, Aldine Publishing Company, Chicago, 1964.

Davis, James A.: "Higher Education: Selection and Opportunity," *The School Review*, **71**:249–265 (Autumn, 1963).

Duncan, Otis Dudley: "Ability and Achievement," *Eugenics Quarterly*, **15**:1–11 (March, 1968).

Duncan, Otis Dudley: "Path Analysis: Sociological Examples," *American Journal of Sociology,* 72:1–16 (July, 1966).

Duncan, Otis Dudley: "A Socioeconomic Index for All Occupations" and "Properties and Characteristics of the Socioeconomic Index," in Albert J. Reiss, Jr. (ed.), *Occupations and Social Status,* The Free Press of Glencoe, Inc., New York, 1961, pp. 109–161.

Duncan, Otis Dudley, David L. Featherman, and Beverly Duncan: *Socioeconomic Background and Occupational Achievement: Extensions of a Basic Model,* Final report, Bureau of Research, Office of Education, U.S. Department of Health, Education, and Welfare, University of Michigan, Ann Arbor, May, 1968.

Feldman, Kenneth A., and Theodore M. Newcomb: *The Impact of College on Students,* vol. 1, *An Analysis of Four Decades of Research,* Jossey-Bass, Inc., San Francisco, 1969.

Flanagan, John C., et al.: *Project Talent: The American High School Student,* Project Talent Office, University of Pittsburgh, 1964.

Flanagan, John C., and William W. Cooley: *Project Talent: One Year Follow-up Studies,* School of Education, University of Pittsburgh, 1966.

Galbraith, John Kenneth: *The New Industrial State,* Houghton Mifflin Company, Boston, 1967.

Gallup Poll releases, May 25, 26, and 27, 1969.

Goodman, Leo A., and William H. Kruskal: "Measures of Association for Cross Classifications," *Journal of the American Statistical Association,* 49:732–764 (December, 1954).

Hodge, Robert W., and Paul M. Siegel: "Methods and Procedures for Rating Occupations," National Opinion Research Center, Chicago, January 1964. Unpublished manuscript.

Hodge, Robert W., Paul M. Siegel, and Peter H. Rossi: "Occupational Prestige in the U.S., 1925–1963," in Reinhard Bendix and Seymour Martin Lipset (eds.), *Class, Status, and Power: Social Stratification in Comparative Perspective,* 2d ed., The Free Press, New York, 1966, pp. 322–334.

Hodge, Robert W., Donald J. Treiman, and Peter H. Rossi: "A Comparative Study of Occupational Prestige," in Reinhard Bendix and Seymour Martin Lipset (eds.), *Class, Status, and Power: Social Stratification in Comparative Perspective,* 2d ed., The Free Press, New York, 1966, pp. 309–321.

Holland, John L.: "Undergraduate Origins of American Scientists," *Science,* 126:433–437 (September 6, 1957).

Inkeles, Alex, and Peter H. Rossi: "National Comparisons of Occupational Prestige," *American Journal of Sociology,* 61:329–339 (January, 1956).

Jencks, Christopher, and David Reisman: *The Academic Revolution,* Doubleday & Company, Inc., Garden City, N.Y., 1968.

Kahn, Herman, and Anthony J. Wiener: "The Next Thirty-three Years: A Framework for Speculation," *Daedalus,* 96:705–732 (Summer, 1967).

Kaplan, Abraham: "The Travesty of the Philosophers," *Change,* 2:12–19 (January–February, 1970).

Katz, Joseph, and associates: *No Time for Youth: Growth and Constraint in College Students,* Jossey-Bass, Inc., San Francisco, 1968.

Miller, Norman: *One Year after Commencement: An Interim Report on the 1961–62 Graduate School Enrollment and the Future Career Plans of the 1961 College Graduating Class,* Report no. 93, National Opinion Research Center, Chicago, June, 1963.

National Opinion Research Center: "Jobs and Occupations: A Popular Evaluation," in Reinhard Bendix and Seymour Martin Lipset (eds.), *Class, Status, and Power: Social Stratification in Comparative Perspective,* 1st ed., The Free Press, New York, 1953, pp. 411–426.

Newman, John Henry: *Idea of a University,* edited by M. J. Svaglic, Holt, Rinehart and Winston, Inc., New York, 1960.

Peterson, Richard E.: *The Scope of Organized Student Protest in 1967–1968,* Educational Testing Service, Princeton, N.J., 1968.

Schwab, Joseph J.: *Curriculum and Student Protest,* The University of Chicago Press, Chicago, 1969.

Servan-Schreiber, J.-J.: *The American Challenge,* translated by Ronald Steel, Atheneum Publishers, New York, 1968.

Smith, Mapheus: "An Empirical Scale of Prestige Status of Occupations," *American Sociological Review,* 8:185–192 (April, 1943).

Spaeth, Joe L.: "The Allocation of College Graduates to Graduate and Professional Schools," *Sociology of Education,* 41:342–349 (Fall, 1968).

Spaeth, Joe L.: "Public Reactions to College Student Protests," *Sociology of Education,* 42:199–206 (Spring, 1969).

Spaeth, Joe L.: *Recent College Graduates,* forthcoming.

Tussman, Joseph: *Experiment at Berkeley,* Oxford University Press, New York, 1969.

Young, Michael: *The Rise of the Meritocracy, 1870–2033,* Random House, Inc., New York, 1959.